Your

German
Vocabulary Guide

for GCSE

Second edition

Val Levick
Glenise Radford
Alasdair McKeane

Titles available
from
Malvern Language Guides:

French	German	Spanish	Italian
Vocabulary Guide	Vocabulary Guide	Vocabulary Guide	Vocabulary Guide
Speaking Test Guide	Speaking Test Guide	Speaking Test Guide	Speaking Test Guide
Essential French Verbs	Esential German Verbs		
Grammar Guide	Grammar Guide	Grammar Guide	Grammar Guide
French Dictionary	German Dictionary		
Mon Echange Scolaire	Mein Austausch	Mi Intercambio Escolar	
Ma Visite En France			
Key Stage 3 Guide	Key Stage 3 Guide	Key Stage 3 Guide	
CE 13+ French			
Standard Grade French			

(Order form inside the back of this book - photocopy and return)

CONTENTS

Please note the following points:

- * These verbs take *sein* in the perfect and other compound tenses.

- *irreg* Irregular (strong) verbs are marked *irreg*.
  There is a table of irregular verbs on pages 91-96.

- *sep* Separable verbs are marked *sep*.

- *insep* These verbs have a prefix which in this instance is inseparable.

- † Regular (weak) verbs which have minor variations are marked †.
  Verbs ending in *-ieren* do not have a *ge-* on the front of the past participle.
  Verbs starting with *be-, emp-, ent-, er-, ge-, ver- and zer-* do not add a *ge-* on the front of the past participle.
  Verbs whose infinitive end in *-den, -men, -nen, and -ten* have the endings *-test* and *-tet* in the *du* and *er* forms of the present tense. In the imperfect tense, they add an extra *e* before the imperfect endings are added. In the perfect tense they add an extra *e* before the final *-t* of the past participle.

- ‡ Adjectival nouns are marked ‡.

- *wk* Weak nouns are marked *wk*.

- *pl* Nouns which only occur in the plural are marked *pl*.

- *no pl* Nouns which have no plural are marked *no pl*.

- *inv* Adjectives which never take an ending are marked *inv* - invariable.

- *coll* Colloquial expressions are marked *coll*.

- Some common words appear in more than one list, if they could be used in more than one situation. Page references are made at the end of sections to indicate other words which might be useful to the topic.

IN DER SCHULE

Anwesenheit   School attendance

die Gesamtschule (n) ... comprehensive school

die Grundschule (n) ..... primary school

das Gymnasium (Gymnasien) .. grammar school

die Hauptschule (n) ..... secondary modern
school

das Internat (e) .... boarding school

der Kindergarten (-gärten) .... nursery school

das Oberstufenkolleg (-kollegien)
.... sixth form college

die private Grundschule (n) ..... prep school

die Privatschule (n)...... public school

die Realschule (n)........ type of secondary
school

die Schule (n) .... (state) school

in der 6. Klasse............ in Year 7

in der 7. Klasse............ in Year 8

in der 8. Klasse............ in Year 9

in der 9. Klasse............ in Year 10

in der 10. Klasse.......... in Year 11

in der 11. Klasse.......... in Year 12

in der 12. Klasse.......... in Year 13

in der Oberstufe.......... in the Sixth Form

Leute   People

der Abiturient (en) *wk* .. sixth former

die Abiturientin (nen) .. sixth former

der Berufsberater (-) .... careers officer

die Berufsberaterin (nen) . careers officer

der Direktor (en).......... secondary school
headmaster

die Direktorin (nen) ..... secondary school
headmistress

der Hausmeister (-) ...... caretaker

der Internatsschüler (-). boarder

die Internatsschülerin (nen) .. boarder

der Klassenkamerad (en) *wk* . classmate

die Klassenkameradin (nen).. classmate

der Klassensprecher (-) class spokesperson

die Klassensprecherin (nen)
.... class spokesperson

der Lehrer (-).............. teacher

die Lehrerin (nen) .... teacher

der Partner (-)............. partner

die Partnerin (nen)....... partner

der Schüler (-) .... pupil

die Schülerin (nen) ...... pupil

der Schulfreund (e)...... school friend

die Schulfreundin (nen)... school friend

die Sekretärin (nen)..... secretary

die SMV...................... school council

der Studienrat (-räte) ... secondary school
teacher

die Studienrätin (nen).. secondary school
teacher

der Tagesschüler (-)..... day-boy

die Tagesschülerin (nen).. day-girl

Das Schulgebäude
The school complex

der Arbeitsraum (-räume) private study room

die Aula (Aulen) .... school hall

die Bibliothek (en) ...... library

das schwarze Brett....... notice board

das Büro (s) .... office

der Fußballplatz (-plätze). football pitch

der Gang (Gänge) .... corridor

die Kantine (n) .... canteen

das Klassenzimmer (-) . classroom

das Labor (s)............... laboratory

das Lazarett (e) .... sick bay

das Lehrerzimmer (-) ... staffroom

der Lehrmittelraum (-räume) .resources centre

das Schwimmbad (-bäder) .....swimming pool

der Schlafraum (-räume).. dormitory

der Schulhof (-höfe) .... playground

das Sprachlabor (s) ...... language lab

der Tagesraum (-räume)
.... pupils' common room

der Tennisplatz (-plätze) .. tennis court

1

die Turnhalle (n)......... gym
der Umkleideraum (-räume) . changing rooms
der Werkraum (-räume) workshop, studio

Das Schuljahr The school year

die Ferien *pl* .... holiday
die Halbjahresferien *pl* February half-term
           holiday
die Herbstferien *pl* .... autumn half-term
           holiday
die Osterferien *pl* .... Easter holiday
die Pfingstferien *pl* ...... summer half-term
           holiday
der Schüleraustausch ... school exchange
das Semester (-) .... semester
die Sommerferien *pl* .... summer holidays
der Stundenplan (-pläne).. timetable
der freie Tag .... day off
das Trimester (-) .... term
der Unterricht .... teaching
die Weihnachtsferien *pl* ... Christmas holidays
die Woche (n)............. week

Der Schultag The school day

die Hausaufgaben *pl* .... homework, prep
das Mittagessen (-) .... midday meal
die Mittagspause (n) .... dinner hour
der Morgen (-) .... morning
der Nachmittag (e) .... afternoon
das Nachsitzen .... detention
die Pause (n)............... break
die Stunde (n) .... lesson
der Tag (e) .... day
die Versammlung (en) . assembly

Die Schuluniform
School uniform

die Bluse (n)............... blouse
das Hemd (en) .... shirt
die Hose (n)................ pair of trousers
die Jacke (n) .... blazer
das Kleid (er) .... dress

der Pulli (s) .... pullover
der Pullover (-) .... pullover
der Rock (Röcke) .... skirt
der Schlips (e) .... tie
der Schuh (e) .... shoe
die Socke (n) .... sock
die Strumpfhose (n)..... pair of tights
die Wolljacke (n)........ cardigan

Wie kommst du zur Schule?
How do you get to school?

mit der Bahn .... by train
mit dem Bus............... by bus
mit dem Rad............... by bicycle
mit dem Schulbus........ by school bus
mit der Straßenbahn .... by tram
mit der U-Bahn .... on the underground
mit dem Wagen.......... by car
zu Fuß........................ on foot

der Bahnhof (-höfe) ..... station
die Bushaltestelle (n) ... bus stop
die U-Bahnstation (en) tube station

Wann kommst du an?
When do you arrive?

früh .... early
pünktlich .... on time
verspätet..................... late
mit Verspätung........... late

Im Klassenzimmer In the classroom

der Bildschirm (e) .... screen
der Computer (-)......... computer
die Decke (n)............... ceiling
die Erlaubnis (se) .... permission
das Fach (Fächer) .... locker, pigeon hole
das Fenster (-)............. window
der Fußboden (-böden) floor
der Kassettenrekorder (-) ..tape recorder
der Kopfhörer.............. headset
die Kreide .... chalk

der Lehrertisch (e) .... teacher's desk
das Mikrophon (e)........ microphone
der Schrank (Schränke) ... cupboard
der Schwamm (Schwämme) . sponge
der Stuhl (Stühle)......... chair
die Tafel (n) .... (black/white) board
der Tageslichtprojektor (en)
.... overhead projector
der Tisch (e) .... table
die Tür (en) .... door
der Videokassettenrekorder (-)
.... video recorder
die Wand (Wände)....... wall (internal)

die Antwort (en) .... reply, answer
der Auszug (-züge) ...... extract
das Beispiel (e) .... example
die Debatte (n)............. debate
der Dialog (e) .... dialogue
das Ergebnis (se).......... result
der Fortschritt (e)........ progress, improvement
die Hausaufgaben *pl* .... homework, prep
die Lektüre .... reading
das Problem (e)........... problem
die Seite (n) .... page
die Sprache (n) .... language
die Stille .... silence
das Symbol (e) .... symbol
die Übung (en) .... exercise
der Unterricht .... teaching
das Wort (e) .... word
das Wort (Wörter)........ (individual) word
die Zeile (n)................ line (in text)

die Aufgabe (n) .... exercise
der Aufsatz (-sätze)...... essay
der Bericht (e)............. report (of event)
der Fehler (-) .... mistake
die Grammatik............. grammar
die Handschrift .... handwriting
der Nebensatz (-sätze).. clause
das Projekt (e)............. project
die Rechtschreibung .... spelling

die Regel (n) .... rule
der Satz (Sätze) .... sentence
die Übersetzung (en) ... translation
die Vokabel (n) .... vocabulary item
der Wortschatz (-schätze) .....vocabulary list
die Zusammenfassung (en) ....summary

Die Ausstattung des Klassenzimmers
Classroom equipment

das Bild (er)................ picture
das Blatt Papier .... sheet of paper
der Bleistift (e) .... pencil
das Buch (Bücher) .... book
das Heft (e)................. exercise book, note
                              book
der Kleber (-) .... glue stick
die Kreide .... chalk
der Kuli (s) .... (ball-point) pen
das Lineal (e).............. ruler
der Ordner (-) .... folder, file, binder
das Papier .... paper
der Radiergummi (s).... rubber
die Schere (n) .... pair of scissors
das Schmierheft (e)...... rough book
der Schreibblock (-blöcke) ....notepad
das Schulbuch (-bücher) ....text book
die Schulmappe (n) ..... schoolbag
der Taschenrechner (-). calculator
das Wörterbuch (-bücher) ......dictionary

die Büroklammer (n) ... paper clip
das Federmäppchen (-) pencil case
der Filzstift (e)............ felt tip pen
der Füller (-)............... (fountain) pen
der Hefter (-) .... stapler; file
die Heftklammer (n).... staple
der Klebstoff (e) .... glue
die Landkarte (n)......... map
der Locher (-) .... hole punch
das Notizbuch (-bücher)... notebook
die Patrone (n)............ ink cartridge
der Pinsel (-)............... paint brush

3

der Ranzen (-)	school bag		

der Ranzen (-)............. school bag
die Reißzwecke (n)...... drawing pin
der Rucksack (-säcke).. rucksack
der Spitzer (-) .... pencil sharpener
der Tesafilm® .... Sellotape®
die Tinte...................... ink
der Tintenlöscher (-).... eraser pen

Die Fächer   School subjects

das Fach (Fächer)......... subject
die Fremdsprache (n)... foreign language
das Lieblingsfach (-fächer) ... favourite subject
die Naturwissenschaft (en).... science

Biologie...................... biology
Chemie........................ chemistry
Deutsch .... German
Englisch .... English
Erdkunde..................... geography
Französisch................. French
Geographie.................. geography
Geschichte.................. history
Kunst........................... art
Mathe(matik).............. maths, mathematics
Musik .... music
Physik .... physics
Religion....................... RS
Spanisch..................... Spanish
Sport .... PE
Technologie................. technology

Betriebswirtschaft........ business studies
Drama .... Expressive Arts
Handarbeit.................. needlework
Informatik .... IT, computer studies
Kochen........................ cookery
Latein.......................... Latin
Medienwissenschaft..... media studies
Textverarbeitung .... word processing
Turnen......................... gymnastics
Wirtschaftslehre .... economics

Prüfungen   Examinations
Noten   Marks

das Abitur................... A Level/GNVQ Level 3
die Abschlussprüfung (en)..... final exam
das Ergebnis (se) .... result
das Halbjahreszeugnis (se).....mid-year report
der Hauptschulabschluss........GNVQ Level 1
die Klassenarbeit (en).. assessment test
die Note (n)................. mark, grade
die Prüfung (en) .... exam
der Realschulabschluss GCSE/GNVQ Level 2
das Zeugnis (se).......... report

1 sehr gut.................. very good
2 gut......................... good
3 befriedigend .... satisfactory
4 ausreichend........... adequate
5 mangelhaft............ weak
6 ungenügend .... unsatisfactory

mündlich .... oral
schriftlich................... written, in writing
bestehen *irreg*............. to pass (an exam)
durchfallen* *sep* .... to fail an exam
sitzen bleiben* *sep* ...... to repeat a year
versetzt werden* *irreg*. to pass the year

Schulvereine und AGs
**   Out of school activities**

die AG (s) .... club
der Ausflug (-flüge)..... trip, outing
der Austausch (e)......... exchange
der Besuch (e) .... visit
die Blaskapelle (n) ...... brass band
der Chor (Chöre) .... choir
der Klub (s) .... club
die Mannschaft (en)..... team
das Orchester (-) .... orchestra
das Spiel (e)................ match
das Theaterstück (e)..... play
das Tournier (e) .... tournament
der Verein (e) .... club

Wie ist die Schule?   What is it like?

alt	old
dumm	stupid
einfach	easy
falsch	wrong
faul	lazy
gut	good
interessant	interesting
jung	young
lang	long
langweilig	boring
Lieblings-	favourite
nett	nice
nicht gut (in)	not good, hopeless (at)
richtig	right, true
Schul-	to do with school
schwach (in)	weak, not good (at)
schwer	difficult
stark (in)	strong, loud, good (at)
super	super
wichtig	important

ausgezeichnet	excellent
fleißig	hard-working
genau	exact, precise
klassisch	classical
kompliziert	complicated
leicht	easy
letzt	last, final
lustig	amusing, funny
modern	modern
neu	new
nützlich	useful
nutzlos	useless
schrecklich	awful
schwierig	difficult
streng	strict
sympathisch	nice

abwesend	absent, away
anwesend	present, here
artig	well-behaved

aus Backstein	of brick
aus Beton	of concrete
böse	naughty
durchschnittlich	average
ehemalig	ex-, former
gemischt	mixed
gesprächig	talkative
gewissenhaft	conscientious

Adverben   Adverbs

gut	well
langsam	slowly
schlecht	badly
schnell	quickly

Nützliche Verben   Useful verbs

antworten †	to reply
aufmachen *sep*	to open
aufschreiben *irreg sep*	to write down
beantworten †	to answer
beginnen *irreg*	to begin
ergänzen †	to complete
fragen (nach + dat)	to ask (for)
hereinkommen* *irreg sep*	to come in
hören	to hear
kopieren †	to copy
lernen	to learn, study at school
lesen *irreg*	to read
Hausaufgaben machen	to do one's homework
öffnen †	to open
schreiben *irreg*	to write
ruhig sein* *irreg*	to be quiet
sprechen *irreg*	to speak
eine Frage stellen	to ask a question
verbessern †	to correct
verstehen *irreg*	to understand
wählen	to choose
wiederholen *insep*	to repeat
zuhören *sep*	to listen (to)
abschreiben *irreg sep*	to copy down
ankreuzen *sep*	to tick (✓)

5

aufpassen *sep* .... to be careful, pay
        attention
aufstehen* *irreg sep* ..... to stand up, to get up
ausfüllen *sep* .... to fill (in)
ausradieren † *sep* .... to rub out, erase
ausschneiden *irreg sep*. to cut out
diskutieren † .... to discuss, chat
durchstreichen *irreg insep* ..... to cross out
entsprechen *irreg* .... to correspond
erklären † .... to explain
auswendig lernen .... to learn by heart
nachsitzen *irreg sep* ..... to be in detention
notieren † .... to note
Notizen machen .... to make notes
ordnen † .... to put in the right order
raten *irreg* .... to guess
rechnen † .... to calculate
singen *irreg* .... to sing
übersetzen *insep* .... to translate
unterstreichen *irreg insep* to underline
vergleichen *irreg* .... to compare
wenden † .... to turn (page)
zählen .... to count
zeichnen † .... to draw
zeigen .... to point out, show
zusehen *irreg sep* .... to look at, watch

ankommen* *irreg sep* .. to arrive
dauern .... to last
denken *irreg* .... to think
sich entschuldigen † .... to apologise
geben *irreg* .... to give
zur Schule gehen* *irreg* ... to go to school
haben *irreg* .... to have
Recht haben *irreg* .... to be right
Unrecht haben *irreg* ..... to be wrong
hassen .... to hate
hinausgehen* *irreg sep* to go out (of)
hineingehen* *irreg sep* to go in
kommen* *irreg* .... to come
können *irreg* .... to be able to, can

ein Experiment machen ....to do an experiment
sagen .... to say, tell
sehen *irreg* .... to see
spielen .... to play
Sport treiben *irreg* ...... to play sport
studieren † .... to study (at university)
tragen *irreg* .... to wear; to carry
unterrichten *insep* .... to teach
vergessen *irreg* .... to forget
verlassen *irreg* .... to leave
verlieren *irreg* .... to lose
Verspätung haben *irreg* to be late
versuchen † .... to try
wissen *irreg* .... to know
wollen *irreg* .... to want to, wish

anwesend sein* *irreg* ... to be present
aufhören *sep* .... to stop
ausfallen* *irreg sep* ..... to be cancelled
beaufsichtigen † .... to supervise
beraten *irreg* .... to advise
bestehen *irreg* .... to get a pass mark
bestrafen † .... to punish
erfinden *irreg* .... to invent
erlauben † .... to allow, give
        permission
fallen lassen *irreg* .... to drop
fehlen .... to be absent
die Anwesenheit feststellen *sep*
        .... to call the register
es handelt sich um ... . it is about ...
herumalbern *sep* .... to play up, mess about
loben .... to praise
Fortschritte machen ..... to make progress
mogeln .... to cheat
nachsitzen *irreg sep* ..... to be in detention
schwänzen .... to skive
sich vorstellen *sep* .... to imagine
vorziehen *irreg sep* ...... to prefer

For further education and training see page 68

Der Lehrer/die Lehrerin sagt:

Kommt/Geht ins Klassenzimmer! *Come/Go into the classroom!*

Mach die Tür/das Fenster zu, bitte! *Close the door/the window, please!*

Setzt euch! *Sit down!*

Ruhig! *Quieten down!*

Ruhe! *Silence!*

Ich stelle die Anwesenheit fest *I'm going to call the register*

Nehmt eure Hefte/eure Ordner heraus! *Get out your exercise books/folders!*

Nehmt das Deutschbuch! *Pick up your German textbook!*

Schlagt Seite 32 auf! *Turn to page 32!*

Lest den Text! *Read the text!*

Sucht ...im Wörterbuch/im Wortschatz! *Look up ... in the dictionary/vocabulary!*

Hört (der Kassette) zu! *Listen (to the tape)!*

Wiederholt! *Repeat!*

Alle noch einmal, bitte! *Once more,everybody!*

Beantwortet die Fragen! *Answer the questions!*

Seit wann lernst du Deutsch? *How long have you been learning German?*

Seht die Tafel an! *Look at the board!*

Den wie vielten haben wir heute? *What is the date today?*

Schreibt das Datum! Heute haben wir den zehnten November *Put the date! It's November 10th*

Schreibt die Überschrift! *Put the title!*

Unterstreicht mit einem Lineal! *Use a ruler to underline!*

Nummeriert von eins bis fünf! *Write the numbers one to five!*

Schreibt Aufgabe 2 zu Ende! *Finish exercise 2!*

Ergänzt die Sätze! *Finish the sentences!*

Verbessert eure Arbeit mit einem grünen Stift! *Correct your work with a green pen!*

Buchstabiere das Wort „Heft"! *Spell the word "Heft"!*

Kreuzt das Kästchen an! *Tick the box!*

Richtig oder falsch? *True or false?*

Such die richtige Antwort heraus! *Choose the right answer!*

Das stimmt! *Right!*

Macht die Hefte zu! *Shut your exercise books!*

Gebt Chris die Hefte, bitte! *Pass the exercise books to Chris, please!*

Sammle die Hefte ein! *Collect up the exercise books!*

Bringt mir eure Hefte ins Lehrerzimmer! *Bring the exercise books to me at the staffroom!*

Der Lehrer/die Lehrerin sagt (Fortsetzung):

Wähl eine Karte, bitte, Chris! *Chris, choose a card, please!*

Such einen Partner/eine Partnerin! *Choose a partner!*

Arbeitet in Zweier-Gruppen! *Work in pairs!*

Arbeite mit deinem Partner/deiner Partnerin! *Work with your partner!*

Bereitet einen Dialog vor! *Work out a dialogue/role play!*

Schreibt die Hausaufgabe in eure Hefte! *Write down the homework in your exercise books!*

Das ist für Dienstag *It's for Tuesday*

Lernt die Vokabeln! *Learn the list of words!*

Das macht ihr für morgen *You will do it for tomorrow*

Das ist für einen Test am kommenden Donnerstag *There will be a test on it next Thursday*

Versteht ihr? *Do you understand?*

Seid ruhig! *Stop talking!*

Beeilt euch! *Hurry up!*

Packt die Sachen weg! *Put your things away!*

Steht auf! *Stand up!*

Stellt die Stühle auf/unter die Tische! *Put the chairs on/under the tables!*

Du sollst mich morgen um neun Uhr im Lehrerzimmer aufsuchen *Come and see me tomorrow morning at 9 in the staffroom*

Der Lehrer/Die Lehrerin korrigiert:

Du hast siebzehn Punkte von zwanzig *You got 17 out of 20*

Du hast nur fünf Punkte von zwanzig *You only got 5 out of 20*

Ausgezeichnet *Excellent*

Sehr gut *Very good*

Gut *Good*

Ziemlich gut *Quite good*

Guter Versuch *Good effort*

Ungenügend *Poor*

Die Schüler/Die Schülerinnen sagen:

Ich lerne seit einem Jahr/seit drei Jahren Deutsch *I've been learning German for one/three years*

Ich verstehe *I understand*

Ich verstehe nicht *I don't understand*

Ich weiß es nicht *I don't know*

Ich habe eine gute/schlechte Note bekommen *I got a good/bad mark*

Sprichst du Deutsch/Englisch? *Do you speak German/English?*

Ich habe mein Heft/meine Hausaufgabe/mein Mäppchen vergessen *I've forgotten my exercise book/my homework/my pencil case*

Ich möchte ein neues Heft, bitte *I would like a new exercise book, please*

Entschuldigen Sie, Herr McKeane/Frau Radford ... *Please Sir/Miss ...*

Auf welcher Seite ist das? *What page are we on?*

Wie sagt man „homework" auf Deutsch? *How do you say "homework" in German?*

Wie schreibt man „der Hund"? *How do you spell "der Hund"?*

Wie heißt „der Hund" auf Englisch? *What does "der Hund" mean in English?*

Wie spricht man das aus? *How do you pronounce that?*

In welches Heft sollen wir das schreiben? *Which exercise book shall we do it in?*

Darf ich das Fenster aufmachen? *May I open the window?*

Darf ich austreten? *May I leave the room?*

Darf ich meinen Bleistift spitzen? *May I sharpen my pencil?*

Darf ich meinen Pullover ausziehen? *May I take off my pullover?*

Ich bin in der achten/neunten/zehnten Klasse *I am in Year 9/10/11*

Redewendungen

Der Unterricht beginnt um neun Uhr und ist um vier Uhr aus *Lessons begin at 9 and end at 4*

Ich habe sechs Stunden pro Tag *I have six lessons a day*

Mein Lieblingsfach ist Erdkunde *My favourite lesson is geography*

Ich bin gut in Geschichte *I am good at history*

Ich bin schlecht in Latein *I am poor at Latin*

Ich bin hoffnungslos in Deutsch *I'm useless at German*

Ich mache meine Prüfungen dieses Jahr *I shall taking my exams this year*

Ich komme um Viertel vor neun in der Schule an *I get to school at 8.45 am*

Ich komme zu Fuß zur Schule *I walk to school*

Ich trage eine Schuluniform *I wear school uniform*

DAS FAMILIENLEBEN

Häuser   Housing

der Bauernhof (-höfe) .. farm

das Doppelhaus (-häuser) . semi-detached house

das Einfamilienhaus (-häuser) .. detached house

das Gebäude (n) .... building

das Haus (Häuser) .... house

das Reihenhaus (-häuser) . terraced house

die Sozialwohnung (en) ... council, housing
                      association flat

das Studio (s) .... bedsit

der Wohnblock (s) .... block of flats

die Wohnung (en) .... flat

Die Gegend   Situation

die Adresse (n) .... address

das Dorf (Dörfer) .... village

der Kreis (e) .... county

das Land .... country (not town)

das Land (Länder) .... region; country; state

das Meer (e) .... sea

die See (n) .... sea

die Stadt (Städte) .... town

das Viertel (-) .... district of town, city

der Vorort (e) .... suburb

im Norden .... in the north

im Osten .... in the east

im Süden .... in the south

im Westen .... in the west

Die Adresse   Address

die Allee (n) .... avenue

die Brücke (n) .... bridge

die Gasse (n) .... passage, alley

die Hauptstraße (n) ...... main road

der Kai (s) .... embankment, quay

der Platz (Plätze) .... square

die Sackgasse (n) .... cul de sac

die Straße (n) .... street, road

der Weg (e) .... lane, path, way

das Zentrum (Zentren) . centre

der Besitzer (-) .... owner

die Besitzerin (nen) ..... owner

die e-mail-Nummer (n) e-mail address

die Faxnummer (n) ...... fax number

die Miete (n) .... rent

die Nummer (n) .... number

die Postleitzahl (en) ..... postcode

die Telefonnummer (n) phone number

der Wohnort (e) .... place of residence

Allgemeines   General

der Aufzug (-züge) ...... lift

die Aussicht (en) .... view

der Balkon (s) .... balcony

der Bewohner (-) .... resident

die Bewohnerin (nen) .. resident

das Dach (Dächer) .... roof

die Decke (n) .... ceiling

der Eingang (-gänge) ... entrance

der Fahrstuhl (-stühle) . lift

das Fenster (-) .... window

der Fußboden (-böden) floor

der Gang (Gänge) .... corridor

die Gartenpforte (n) ..... gate

das Geländer (-) .... banisters

das Glas .... glass

der Griff (e) .... handle

die Haustür (e) .... (front) door

der Kamin (e) .... fireplace, chimney

der Lift (s) .... lift

die Mauer (n) .... wall (external)

der Mieter (-) .... tenant

die Mieterin (nen) .... tenant

der Plan (Pläne) .... plan

der Quadratmeter (-) .... square metre

das Regal (e) .... shelf

der Rollladen (-läden) .. shutter

das Schloss (Schlösser) lock

der Schlüssel (-).......... key
der Stock (-) .... floor, storey
die Stufe (n) .... step (on stairs)
die Treppe (n)............. staircase
der Treppenflur (e) ...... landing
die Wand (Wände)....... wall (internal)

im Erdgeschoss............ on the ground floor
im Keller..................... in the cellar
oben .... upstairs
im ersten Stock............ on the first floor
unten .... downstairs

der Anstrich................. paint(ing)
das Gas........................ gas
die Glühbirne (n)......... light bulb
der Heizkörper (-)........ radiator
das Putzen................... cleaning
der Schalter (-)............ switch
die Steckdose (n)......... plug
der Strom..................... electricity
das Wasser................... water
die Zentralheizung....... central heating

Die Zimmer　　　Rooms

das Arbeitszimmer (-) .. study
das Badezimmer (-)...... bathroom
der Dachboden (-böden) .. attic, loft
die Diele (n) .... hall
das Esszimmer (-) .... dining room
die Garage (n).............. garage (domestic)
der Hausflur (e) .... hall
der Keller (-)................ cellar, basement
das Kinderzimmer (-)... playroom
das Klo (s) .... toilet, loo
die Küche (n)............... kitchen
das Schlafzimmer (-).... bedroom
der Speicher (-)........... attic, loft
die Terrasse (n)............ patio, terrace
die Toilette (n)............. toilet
die Waschküche (n) ..... utility room
der Wintergarten (-gärten) .... conservatory
das Wohnzimmer (-) .... living-room, lounge

Das Bad　　　　　**Bathroom**
das Bad....................... bath (activity)
das Badetuch (-tücher). bath towel
die Badewanne (e)....... bath (tub)
das Bidet (s)................ bidet
das Deo (s) .... deodorant
die Dusche (n) .... shower
das Handtuch (-tücher) towel
der Rasierapparat (e).... razor
das Schaumbad........... bubble bath
der Schwamm (Schwämme) ..sponge
die Seife...................... soap
der Shampoo (s) .... shampoo
der Spiegel (-) .... mirror
das Toilettenpapier ...... toilet paper
das Waschbecken (-).... wash basin
der Waschlappen (-) .... flannel
heißes Wasser........ hot water
kaltes Wasser......... cold water
der Wasserhahn (-hähne) . tap
die Zahnbürste (n) .... toothbrush
die Zahnpasta .... toothpaste

Das Schlafzimmer　　**Bedroom**
das Bett (en) .... bed
der Bezug (Bezüge) ..... duvet cover
das Buch (Bücher) .... book
die CD (s)................... compact disc
der Computer (-)......... computer
der Fernseher (-)......... television set
der Föhn (e)................ hairdryer
die Gardine (n) .... net curtain
die Haarbürste (n)........ brush
der Kamm (Kämme).... comb
die Kassette (n) .... cassette
der Kleiderschrank (-schränke) ... wardrobe
das Kopfkissen (-)........ pillow
das Laken (-) .... sheet
die Lampe (n)............. lamp
das Poster (-) .... poster
der Radiowecker (-) ..... radio clock
der Sessel (-) .... easy chair
der Spiegel (-) .... mirror

11

das Spielzeug *no pl* ...... toys
die Steppdecke (n) .... duvet, quilt
die Stereoanlage (n) ..... stereo system
der Stuhl (Stühle) .... chair (hard)
der Teppich (e) .... rug, carpet (not fitted)
der Teppichboden (böden) .... fitted carpet
das Videospiel (e) .... video game
der Vorhang (-hänge)... curtain
der Walkman® (Walkmen)... personal stereo
die Wolldecke (n) .... blanket

Das Wohnzimmer   **Living room, Lounge**
der Aschenbecher (-) ... ashtray
das Bücherregal (e) ...... book-case
die CD (s) .... compact disc
der CD-Spieler (-) .... CD player
der Couchtisch (e)........ coffee table
der Fernseher (-) .... TV set
das Foto (s) .... photo
das Gemälde (-) .... painting
der Kamin (e) .... fireplace
der Kassettenrekorder (-) . cassette recorder
das Kissen (-) .... cushion
das Klavier (e) .... upright piano
der Sessel (-)................ armchair
das Sofa (s) .... sofa, settee
die Stereoanlage (-) ..... stereo system
der Teppichboden (-böden)... fitted carpet
die Uhr (en) .... clock
der Videokassettenrekorder (-)
.... video recorder

Das Eßzimmer   **Dining room**
die Anrichte (n) .... sideboard
das Besteck .... cutlery
die Gabel (n) .... fork
das Geschirr................ crockery
das Glas (Gläser) .... glass
die Kaffeekanne (n)..... coffee pot
die Kerze (n) .... candle
der Korkenzieher (-) .... corkscrew
der Löffel (-) .... spoon
das Messer (-) .... knife

die Schüssel (n).......... bowl
der Stuhl (Stühle) .... chair
die Tasse (n)................ cup
die Teekanne (n) .... teapot
der Teller (-)............... plate
der Tisch (e) .... table
die Tischdecke (n)....... tablecloth
die Untertasse (n) .... saucer

Die Küche   **Kitchen**
der Abfalleimer (-) ...... rubbish bin
die Bratpfanne (n) .... frying pan
das Bügelbrett (er) .... ironing board
das Bügeleisen (-)........ iron
der Dosenöffner (-)...... can opener
der Elektroherd (e) ...... electric cooker
der Flaschenöffner (-).. bottle opener
der Gasherd (e)........... gas cooker
der Kühlschrank (-schränke)..fridge
der Mikrowellenherd (e)...microwave (oven)
der Ofen (Öfen).......... oven
der Schnellkochtopf (-töpfe)..pressure cooker
der Schrank (Schränke) cupboard
das Spülbecken (-) .... sink
die Spülmaschine (n)... dishwasher
der Staubsauger (-) ...... vacuum cleaner
die Streichhölzer *pl* ..... matches
das Tablett (s) .... tray
die Tiefkühltruhe (n) ... freezer
der Toaster (-) .... toaster
der Topf (Töpfe) .... saucepan
die Trockenschleuder (-n) .....spin dryer
der Wäschetrockner (-) tumble dryer
die Waschmaschine (n) washing machine

Die Diele   **Hall**
der Anrufbeantworter (-) ..answering machine
der Eingang (-gänge)... entrance
die Haustür (en) .... front door
die Klingel (n)............. doorbell
der Schlüssel (-) .... key
das Telefon (e)............. telephone
die Treppe................. staircase

Die Garage — Garage

das Auto (s) .... car
das Fahrrad (-räder) ..... bike
das Motorrad (-räder) ... motorbike
das Rad (Räder) .... bike
der Rasenmäher (-) ...... lawnmower
der Roller (-) .... scooter
der Wagen (-) .... car
das Werkzeug *no pl* ...... tools

Der Garten — Garden

der Abstellplatz (-plätze) .. parking space
der Apfelbaum (-bäume) .. apple tree
der Baum (Bäume) .... tree
die Blume (n) .... flower
das Blumenbeet (e) ...... flower bed
der Busch (Büsche) ...... bush
das Gemüse .... vegetable
der Gemüsegarten (-gärten) .. vegetable garden
die Gemüsesorte (n) ..... type of vegetable
das Gewächshaus (-häuser) ... greenhouse
das Gras .... grass
die Hecke (n) .... hedge
das Obst .... fruit
der Obstbaum (-bäume) .... fruit tree
die Obstsorte (n) .... type of fruit
die Pflanze (n) .... plant
der Rasen (-) .... lawn
die Schubkarre (n) .... wheelbarrow
der Schuppen (-) .... shed
der Strauch (Sträucher) shrub
die Tanne (n) .... fir tree
die Terrasse (n) .... patio, terrace

Wie ist das Haus? — What is it like?

angenehm .... pleasant
bequem .... comfortable
eigen .... own
elegant .... elegant
freundlich .... welcoming
gemütlich .... cosy
groß .... big
hässlich .... ugly

hübsch .... pretty
klein .... small
modern .... modern
neu .... new
oben .... upstairs
perfekt .... perfect
praktisch .... practical
privat .... private
ruhig .... quiet, peaceful
sauber .... clean
schick .... smart
schmutzig .... dirty
schön .... beautiful
teuer .... dear, expensive
unten .... downstairs

eng .... narrow
funkelnagelneu .... brand new
laut .... noisy
leer .... empty
luxuriös .... luxurious
möbliert .... furnished
notwendig .... necessary
seltsam .... odd, strange
unentbehrlich .... essential
vornehm .... posh
in gutem Zustand .... in good condition
in schlechtem Zustand . in poor condition

ehemalig .... ex-, former
industriell .... industrial
malerisch .... picturesque
touristisch .... tourist
typisch .... typical

Wo ist es? — Where is it?

mit Blick auf den Garten . overlooking the garden
mit Blick auf die Straße ... overlooking the street
im Erdgeschoss .... on the ground floor
unten .... downstairs
oben .... upstairs
hier lang .... this way, that way

auf (+ dat) .... on
hinter (+ dat) .... behind
in (+ dat) .... in
unter (+ dat) .... under
vor (+ dat) .... in front of
zwischen (+ dat) .... between

Nützliche Verben   **Useful verbs**
den Tisch abräumen *sep* ... to clear the table
anmachen *sep* .... to light, switch on
im Garten arbeiten † ... to garden
aufräumen *sep* .... to tidy up
ausmachen *sep* .... to switch off
brauchen .... to need
den Tisch decken .... to set the table
einkaufen *sep* .... to do the shopping
helfen *irreg* (+ dat) ...... to help
kaufen .... to buy
kochen .... to cook, boil
das Bett machen .... to make the bed
Hausarbeit machen ...... to do housework
die Wäsche machen ..... to do the washing
den Rasen mähen .... to mow the lawn
öffnen † .... to open
putzen .... to clean
reparieren † .... to repair
schließen *irreg* .... to shut
spülen .... to do the washing up
teilen .... to share
vorbereiten † *sep* .... to prepare (eg food)
wischen .... to wipe
wohnen .... to live, reside

anbauen *sep* .... to extend (house)
anschließen *irreg sep* ... to plug in
anstreichen *irreg sep* .... to paint, decorate
aufdrehen *sep* .... turn on tap
backen *irreg* .... to bake
basteln .... to do odd jobs, DIY
begiessen *irreg* .... to water
begrüssen † .... to greet, welcome
braten *irreg* .... to fry, roast

bügeln .... to iron
klingeln .... to ring (the doorbell)
klopfen .... to knock on the door
möblieren † .... to furnish
staubsaugen .... to vacuum
tapezieren † .... to wallpaper
umbauen *sep* .... to convert (house)
umkippen *sep* .... to upset, overturn
umziehen* *irreg sep* .... to move house
zudrehen *sep* .... turn off tap

sich anziehen *irreg sep* to get dressed
aufstehen* *irreg sep* .... to get up
aufwachen* *sep* .... to wake up
sich die Haare bürsten † ...to brush one's hair
einschlafen* *irreg sep*.. to fall asleep
ins Bett gehen* *irreg* ... to go to bed
sich kämmen .... to comb one's hair
sich die Zähne putzen.. to clean one's teeth
sich rasieren † .... to shave
sich waschen *irreg* ...... to wash oneself

essen *irreg* .... to eat
zu Abend essen *irreg* ... to have evening meal
zu Mittag essen *irreg* ... to have lunch
frühstücken .... to have breakfast
Durst haben *irreg* .... to be thirsty
Hunger haben *irreg* ..... to be hungry
trinken *irreg* .... to drink

abfahren* *irreg sep* ...... to leave, depart
abholen *sep* .... to meet, pick up
ankommen* *irreg sep* . to arrive
verlassen *irreg* .... to leave (place)

For meals see page 23
For food and drink see page 53
For pets see page 30
For weekend activities and hobbies see page 32
For expressing opinions see page 39
For colours see page 29
For times see page 90

Redewendungen

Wo wohnst du? *Where do you live?*

Was gibt es in deinem Schlafzimmer? *What is there in your bedroom?*

In meinem Zimmer habe ich ein Bett, einen Tisch, einen Computer und eine Lampe *I have a bed, a table, a computer and a lamp in my room*

Ich wohne im Erdgeschoss *I live on the ground floor*

Was machst du zu Hause? *What do you do at home?*

Ich spüle *I do the washing up*

Mein Bruder geht mit dem Hund spazieren *My brother takes the dog for a walk*

Als Gast   Being a guest

der Brieffreund (e) .... penfriend (m)
die Brieffreundin (nen) penfriend (f)
der Gast (Gäste) .... guest (m)
der Gastgeber (-) .... host
die Gastgeberin (nen) .. hostess

das Geschenk (e) .... present
der Koffer (-) .... suitcase
die Reisetasche (n) .... holdall
die Seife .... soap
das Shampoo .... shampoo
die Wolldecke (n) .... blanket
die Zahnbürste (n) .... toothbrush
die Zahnpasta .... toothpaste

älter .... elder, older
deutsch .... German
englisch .... English
freundlich .... welcoming
glücklich..................... pleased
interessant.................. interesting
irisch .... Irish
jünger .... younger

nett .... nice
schottisch .... Scottish
schüchtern .... shy
sympathisch................ kind
walisisch .... Welsh

Nützliche Verben   Useful verbs

abfahren* *irreg sep* ...... to leave, depart
ankommen* *irreg sep* .. to arrive
ausgehen* *irreg sep* ..... to go out
ausleihen *irreg sep* .... to borrow
brauchen..................... to need
Deutsch sprechen *irreg* to speak German
Englisch sprechen *irreg* to speak English
essen *irreg* .... to eat
finden *irreg* .... to find
helfen *irreg* (+ dat) ...... to help
können *irreg*............... to be able to
lächeln........................ to smile
leihen *irreg*................. to lend
schenken .... to give (present)
vergessen *irreg* .... to forget
willkommen heißen *irreg* to welcome

Redewendungen

Ich habe meinen Waschlappen vergessen *I have forgotten my flannel*

Wo ist das Badezimmer, bitte? *Where is the bathroom, please?*

Darf ich bitte meinen Vater anrufen? *May I phone my father, please?*

Wir essen gegen acht Uhr *We have our evening meal at about 8 pm*

DIE MEDIEN

Allgemeines　　　General

das Fernsehen .... television
das Kino (s) .... cinema
die Presse .... press
das Radio .... radio
das Theater (-) .... theatre

Im Kino　　　　At the cinema

der Charakter (e) .... character
der Film (e) .... film
die Handlung (en) .... plot
der Held (en) *wk* .... hero
die Heldin (nen) .... heroine
die Nachmittagsvorstellung (en)
.... afternoon performance
das Programm (e) .... TV station
der Schauspieler (-) ...... actor
die Schauspielerin (nen) .. actress
der Schurke (n) *wk* ...... villain
die Sendung (en) .... TV programme
der Star (s) .... filmstar
der Untertitel (-) .... subtitle
die Vorstellung (en) ..... (film) showing

Was gibt es?　　　What's on?

der Abenteuerfilm (e) .. adventure film
der Gruselfilm (e) .... horror film
der Horrorfilm (e) .... horror film
die Komödie (n) .... comedy film
der Krimi (s) .... detective film
der Liebesfilm (e) .... love film
der Science-Fiction-Film (e) . science fiction
　　　　　　　　　　　　　　film
der Spielfilm (e) .... feature film
der Spionagefilm (e) .... spy film
der Thriller (s) .... thriller
der Western (s) .... Western
der Zeichentrickfilm (e)... cartoon

Die Presse　　　The press

der Leser (-) .... reader

die Leserin (nen) .... reader
der Zeitungshändler (-) .newsagent
der Zeitungskiosk (e) ....news stand

der Artikel (-) .... article
der Bericht (e) .... report
der Comic (s) .... comic strip
die Frauenzeitschrift (en) . women's magazine
die Illustrierte (n) ‡ ..... illustrated magazine
die Kleinanzeige (n) ..... small ad
das Kreuzworträtsel (-) . crossword
die Lektüre .... reading
die Modezeitschrift (en) ... fashion magazine
die Nachrichtenzeitschrift (en)
.... news magazine
die Schlagzeile (n) .... headline
die Sportnachrichten *pl* sports page
die Tageszeitung (en) ... daily paper
der Wetterbericht (e) .... weather report
die Wochenzeitschrift (en)
.... weekly paper, magazine
die Zeitschrift (en) .... magazine
die Zeitung (en) .... newspaper

Im Radio　　　On the radio
Im Fernsehen　　On TV

die Band (s) .... group, band
die Gruppe (n) .... group
der Komödiant (en) *wk* . comedian
die Komödiantin (en) ... comedienne
der Moderator (en) .... presenter

die Dokumentarsendung (en) ... documentary
die Fernbedienung .... remote control,
　　　　　　　　　　　　　　zapper
das Kabelfernsehen .... cable TV
die Krimiserie (n) .... police series
die Nachrichten *pl* .... news
das Nachrichtenmagazin ... news show
das Programm (e) .... channel
die Quizsendung (en) ... quiz show
die Reklame (n) .... advert

16

die Satellitenschüssel (n) . satellite dish
die Seifenoper (n) .... soap opera
die Sendung (en) .... programme, broadcast
die Serie (n) .... series
die Sportsendung (en).. sports broadcast
die Talkshow (s) .... a talk show
das Theaterstück (e) ..... play
die Videokassette (n) ... video cassette
der Videorekorder (-) ... video recorder
die Wettervorhersage (n) . weather forecast

Die Musik   Music

die CD (s) .... compact disc, CD
der CD-Spieler (-) .... CD player
die klassische Musik .... classical music
der Jazz .... jazz
der Kassettenrekorder (-) . cassette recorder
die Popmusik .... pop music
der Rap .... rap
der Rock .... rock
der Sänger (-) .... singer
die Stereoanlage (n) ..... stereo system
der Walkman® (Walkmen)... walkman ®

Das Theater   The theatre

das Ballett (e) .... ballet
das Drama (Dramen).... drama
die Handlung (en) .... plot
die Komödie (n) .... comedy
die Oper (n) .... opera
das Publikum .... audience
das Theaterstück (e) ..... play
die Tragödie (n) .... tragedy
die Truppe (n) .... theatre company
die Vorstellung (en) ..... performance

Wann hast du das gesehen?
When did you see/hear it?
am Abend .... in the evening
am Morgen .... in the morning
am Nachmittag .... in the afternoon
am Wochenende .... at the weekend

gestern .... yesterday
heute .... today
heute Morgen .... this morning
letzte Woche .... last week
vor drei Tagen .... three days ago
vor einem Monat .... a month ago
vorgestern .... the day before yesterday

Wo hast du das gesehen?
Where did you see/hear it?
auf CD .... on CD
auf Kassette .... on tape
auf Video .... on video
im Fernsehen .... on television
im Jugendklub .... at the youth club
im Kino .... at the cinema
im Konzert .... at a concert
im Radio .... on the radio
im Theater .... at the theatre

Wie ist es?   **What is it like?**
aufregend .... exciting
außergewöhnlich .... extraordinary
ausgezeichnet .... excellent
berühmt .... famous
echt gut .... super
eindrucksvoll .... impressive
einmalig .... superb
ernst .... serious
furchtbar .... dreadful
gewöhnlich .... usually
gut .... good
hervorragend .... excellent
interessant .... interesting
jung .... young
klasse .... super
klassisch .... classical
komisch .... funny
kurz .... short
lächerlich .... ridiculous
lang .... long
langweilig .... boring
Lieblings- .... favourite

17

lustig .... amusing, funny

monatlich .... monthly

neust........................... last, latest

nutzlos....................... useless

im Originalton .... with the original
                 soundtrack

Pop˷ .... pop

prima.......................... very good, super

(nicht) schlecht........... (not) bad

schlimm...................... bad

schön.......................... nice

schrecklich .... awful

seltsam .... funny (odd)

sensationell................. sensational

spannend .... exciting

super........................... very good, super

synchronisiert .... dubbed

täglich .... daily

tragisch....................... tragic

unangenehm .... unpleasant

mit Untertiteln .... sub-titled

widerlich .... revolting

wöchentlich................. weekly

Nützliche Verben   Useful verbs

sich amüsieren † .... to have a good time

anfangen *irreg sep* .... to begin

anmachen *sep* .... to switch on

aufnehmen *irreg sep* .... to record

ausmachen *sep*............ to switch off

beginnen *irreg* .... to begin

dauern .... to last

enden † ....to end

finden *irreg* ....to find

genießen *irreg* ....to enjoy

lieber haben *irreg*........to prefer

es handelt sich um........it is about

hassen ....hate

hören...........................to hear

sich interessieren für (+ acc) †
             ....to be interested in

können *irreg* ....to be able to, can

lachen ....to laugh

lesen *irreg* ....to read

lieben...........................to like a lot

meinen.........................to think

mögen *irreg* ....to like

schätzen ....to appreciate

sehen *irreg* ....to see

singen *irreg*.................to sing

spielen.........................to play

telefonieren † ....to phone

verachten † ....to despise

vergleichen *irreg*.........to compare

vorziehen *irreg sep*.......to prefer

wählen ....to choose

zuhören *sep* ....to listen (to)

zusehen *irreg sep* ....to watch

For words to express an opinion see pages 39, 41

For days of the week see page 89

For buying tickets see page 35

For advertising see page73

Redewendungen

Gehen wir ins Kino? *Shall we go to the cinema?*

Was läuft? *What's on?*

Ich mag Abenteuerfilme *I like adventure films*

Ich höre gern Musik *I like listening to music*

Ich interessiere mich für Jazz *I'm interested in jazz*

Ich habe eine CD-Sammlung *I have a collection of CDs*

Wie hast du den Film gefunden? *What did you think of the film?*

Ich habe ihn spannend gefunden *I thought it was exciting*

Wo hast du es gehört/gesehen? *Where did you hear/see it?*

18

GESUNDHEIT UND FITNESS

Die Körperteile   Parts of the body

der Arm (e) .... arm
das Auge (n) .... eye
das Bein (e) .... leg
der Finger (-) .... finger
der Fuß (Füße) .... foot
das Gesicht (er) .... face
das Haar (e) .... hair
der Hals (Hälse) .... throat
die Hand (Hände) .... hand
das Knie (-) .... knee
der Kopf (Köpfe) .... head
der Mund (Münder) ..... mouth
die Nase (n) .... nose
das Ohr (en) .... ear
der Rücken (-) .... back

die Brust (Brüste) .... chest, bust, breast
der Daumen (-) .... thumb
der Ellenbogen (-) .... elbow
der Fingernagel (nägel) finger nail
das Fußgelenk (e) .... ankle
die Gesichtszüge *pl* ..... features
das Glied (er) .... limb
das Handgelenk (e) ...... wrist
die Haut (Häute) .... skin
die Hüfte (n) .... hip
das Kinn (e) .... chin
die Lippe (n) .... lip
der Nacken (-) .... nape of neck
der Oberschenkel (-) .... thigh
die Schulter (n) .... shoulder
die Stimme (n) .... voice
die Stirn (en) .... forehead
die Taille (n) .... waist
die Wange (n) .... cheek
der Zeh (en) .... toe

der Bauch (Bäuche) ..... stomach
das Blut .... blood

das Gehirn (e) .... brain
das Herz (en) *wk* .... heart
der Knochen (-) .... bone
die Leber (n) .... liver
die Lunge (n) .... lungs
der Magen (-) .... stomach
der Muskel (-n) .... muscle
die Niere (n) .... kidney
die Rippe (n) .... rib
der Zahn (Zähne) .... tooth
die Zunge (n) .... tongue

Leute   People

der Apotheker (-) .... chemist
die Apothekerin (nen).. chemist
der Arzt (Ärzte) .... doctor
die Ärztin (nen) .... doctor
der Krankenpfleger (-). nurse
die Krankenschwester (n) nurse
der Optiker (-) .... optician
die Optikerin (nen) ...... optician
der Patient (en) *wk* ...... patient
die Patientin (nen) .... patient
der Physiotherapeut (en) *wk*...physiotherapist
die Physiotherapeutin (nen) ...physiotherapist
der Psychiater (-) .... psychiatrist
die Psychiaterin (nen).. psychiatrist
der Psychologe (n) *wk* . psychologist
die Psychologin (nen).. psychologist
der Sozialarbeiter (-).... social worker
die Sozialarbeiterin (nen) social worker
der Zahnarzt (-ärzte) .... dentist
die Zahnärztin (nen) .... dentist

Krankheiten   Health problems

der Biss .... bite (eg dog)
der Durchfall .... diarrhoea
die Erkältung.............. cold
das Fieber .... fever, high temperature
die Grippe .... flu

der Heuschnupfen........ hay fever

der Husten.................. cough

der Insektenstich (e)..... insect sting, bite

die Kopfschmerzen *pl*.. headache

die Magenverstimmung.... indigestion

die Mandelentzündung..... tonsillitis

die Masern *pl*.............. measles

die Mumps.................. mumps

die Röteln *pl*............... German measles

der Schnupfen.............. cold

die Schwellung (en)..... swelling

die Seekrankheit.......... sea-sickness

der Sonnenstich.......... sunstroke

die Tage *pl*................. period

die Verstauchung (en).. sprain

die Windpocken *pl*...... chicken pox

Beim Arzt   At the doctor's
Beim Zahnarzt   At the dentist's

die AOK...................... sickness insurance
                                     scheme

das Attest (e)................ doctor's certificate

die Behandlung (en).... treatment

die Brille (n)............... pair of glasses

der E111-Schein (e)..... E111

die erste Hilfe.............. first aid

der Gips...................... plaster (broken bones)

die Klinik (en)............. clinic

die Kosten *pl*.............. expenses, cost

der Krankenwagen (-).. ambulance

die Krankheit (en)....... illness

das Mal (e).................. time, occasion

das Medikament (e)..... medicine

das Mittel.................... remedy

die Operation (en)....... operation

die Plombe (n)............. filling

die Praxis (Praxen)...... surgery

das Problem (e)........... problem

das Rezept (e).............. prescription

das Röntgenbild (er).... X-ray

der Schmerz (en)......... pain

die Spritze (n)............. injection

der Termin (e)............. appointment

die Versicherung (en).. insurance

In der Apotheke   At the chemist's

die Antibiotika *pl*........ antibiotics

    Aspirin®............... aspirin®

die Creme.................... cream

die Damenbinde (n)..... sanitary towel

das Dragée (s)............. capsule

das Fieber................... temperature

das Hansaplast®......... plaster, elastoplast®

der Hustenbonbon (s) .. throat sweet

der Hustensaft (-säfte) . cough mixture

der Löffel (-)............... spoonful

der Saft (Säfte)........... (liquid) medicine

die Salbe (n)............... cream, balm

die Seife..................... soap

der Sonnenbrand.......... sunburn

die Tablette (n)........... tablet

der Tampon (s)........... tampon

das Tempotaschentuch®...tissue

die Tube (n) .... tube

der Verband (-bände)... dressing

die Watte.................... cotton wool

die Zahnpasta............. toothpaste

das Zäpfchen (-)......... suppository

ausfüllen *sep* .... to fill in

sich ausruhen *sep*........ to rest

einen Termin ausmachen *sep*

.... to make an appointment

beißen *irreg*............... to bite

besuchen † .... to go and see

bezahlen † .... to pay (for)

im Bett bleiben* *irreg* . to stay in bed

einspritzen *sep*............ to inject (a drug)

sich krank fühlen......... to feel ill

sich wohl fühlen.......... to feel well

ins Bett gehen* *irreg* ... to go to bed

eine Erkältung haben *irreg* ....to have a cold

Fieber haben............... to have a raised
                                     temperature

Halsschmerzen haben .. to have a sore throat

Kopfschmerzen haben . ... to have a headache
Magenschmerzen haben... to have stomach-ache
Ohrenschmerzen haben ... to have earache
Rückenschmerzen haben.. to have backache
Zahnschmerzen haben . ... to have toothache
husten † .... to cough
impfen .... to immunise
Fieber messen *irreg* ..... to take someone's
　　　　　　　　　　　　temperature
niesen .... to sneeze
schwitzen .... to sweat
stechen *irreg* .... to sting
warten † .... to wait (for)
zittern .... to shiver

Das gesunde Leben　Healthy lifestyle

die Aerobik .... aerobics
der Alkohol .... alcohol
die Biokost .... organic foods
die Biokultur .... organic farming
die Droge (n) .... drug
der Drogensüchtige (n) ‡ . drug addict
die Fast Food-Industrie fast food industry
das Fett .... fat
der Fettgehalt .... fat content
der Fitness .... fitness
das Fitnessprogramm ... work-out
das Gemüse .... vegetables
das Molkereiprodukt (e)... dairy product
die Nahrung .... food
das Obst .... fruit
der Raucher (-) .... smoker
der Schlaf .... sleep
der Stress .... stress
die Süßigkeiten *pl* .... sweet things
der Tabak .... tobacco
die Trunkenheit .... drunkenness (habitual)
die Vitamine *pl* .... vitamins

das Aids .... AIDS
das Amphetamin .... amphetamines
der Bluthochdruck .... high blood pressure

die Bulimie .... bulimia
das Heroin .... heroin
das Insektizid (e) .... insecticide
der Junkie (s) .... junkie
der Kunstdünger (-) ..... chemical fertiliser
die Magersucht .... anorexia
der Schnüffler (-) .... glue sniffer
die Überdosis (-dosen). overdose

abnehmen *irreg sep* ..... to lose weight
aufhören *sep* .... to stop
aufstehen* *irreg sep* .... to get up
sich entspannen † .... to relax
essen *irreg* .... to eat
das Recht haben *irreg* .. to have the right (to)
laufen* *irreg* .... to run
Diät machen .... to go on a diet
Drogen nehmen *irreg* .. to take drugs
Drogen probieren † ..... to try drugs
raten *irreg* (+ dat) .... to advise
rauchen .... to smoke
respektieren † .... to respect
schlafen *irreg* .... to sleep
sich trainieren † .... to train
superfit sein* *irreg* ...... to be very fit
vermeiden *irreg* .... to avoid
sich waschen *irreg* .... to wash
werden* *irreg* .... to become
zunehmen *irreg sep* ..... to put on weight

Was ist los?　　What's the matter?

allergisch (gegen + acc)... allergic (to)
asthmatisch .... asthmatic
behindert .... handicapped
betrunken .... drunk
dringend .... urgent
erkältet .... having a cold
erstaunlich .... surprising
fett .... fat, fatty
geschwollen .... swollen
gesund .... healthy, in good health
heiß .... hot

kalt .... cold
krank ill
magersüchtig .... anorexic
müde .... tired
nass .... wet
sauber .... clean
schläfrig .... sleepy
schmutzig .... dirty
schwach .... weak
sicher .... certain, sure
ungesund .... in poor health
unwohl .... unwell
vegan .... vegan
vegetarisch .... vegetarian
wahr .... true
zuckerkrank .... diabetic

Ist es ernst?   Is it serious?

ängstlich .... anxious
ernst .... serious
erschöpft .... exhausted
falsch .... false, wrong
langsam .... slowly
im Schock .... in shock
tot .... dead
bewusstlos .... unconscious
vergiftet .... poisoned
verletzt .... injured
schwer verletzt .... seriously injured

Nützliche Verben   Useful verbs

aufpassen *sep* .... to pay attention
sich beeilen † .... to hurry
bluten † .... to bleed
sich den Arm brechen *irreg* ...to break one's arm
sich entschuldigen † .... to apologize
sich erbrechen *irreg* ..... to vomit
Angst haben *irreg* .... to be afraid, worried
helfen *irreg* (+dat) .... to help
hinfallen* *irreg sep* ..... to fall
informieren † .... to inform
ins Krankenhaus kommen* *irreg*
.... to go into hospital
protestieren † .... to protest
rufen *irreg* .... to call
sich in den Finger schneiden *irreg*
.... to cut one's finger
schreien *irreg* .... to shout
töten † .... to kill
umkippen *sep* .... to knock, turn over
sich verbrennen *irreg* ... to burn
sich verletzen † .... to hurt oneself,
                          be injured
sich das Fußgelenk verstauchen †
.... to sprain one's ankle
weinen .... to cry (weep)
böse werden* *irreg* ...... to get angry
zusehen *irreg sep* .... watch, look at

For sport etc see page 34
For food and drink see pages 23, 53

Redewendungen

Was ist los? *What is the matter?*

Ich habe mir das Bein gebrochen *I've broken my leg*

Ich habe Fieber *I've got a high temperature*

Eine Mücke hat mich gestochen *A mosquito has stung me*

Ich fühle mich unwohl *I feel sick*

Haben Sie etwas gegen Husten? *Have you anything for a cough?*

Gute Besserung! *Get well soon!*

ESSEN UND TRINKEN

Die Mahlzeiten   Meals

das Abendessen (-) .... dinner, evening meal
das Essen (-) .... food
das Frühstück (e) .... breakfast
der Imbiss (-e) .... snack
Kaffee und Kuchen afternoon coffee
das Mittagessen (-) .... lunch, midday meal
das Picknick (s) .... picnic
der Schnellimbiss (-imbisse) . take-away meal

Wo geht man essen?
Where are you going to eat?

die Bar (s) .... bar
die Bierhalle (n) .... beer hall
das Café (s) .... café
das Gasthaus (-häuser) . pub, inn
der Gasthof (-höfe) ...... pub, inn
die Gaststätte (n) .... pub
die Imbissstube (n) ...... fast food restaurant, snack bar
das Kaffeehaus (-häuser).. coffee bar
die Kneipe (n) .... pub
die Konditorei (en) ...... café; cake shop
die Pizzeria (s) .... pizzeria
der Ratskeller (-) .... town hall cellar restaurant
das Restaurant (s) .... restaurant
der Schnellimbiss (-e) .. snack bar
das Stehcafé (s) .... quick café
die Trinkhalle (n) .... drinks stand
die Weinstube (n) .... wine bar
die Wirtschaft (en) .... pub
das Wirtshaus (-häuser) hotel
die Wurstbude (n) .... sausage stand

Im Restaurant   In a restaurant

Leute   People

der Inhaber (-) .... owner
die Inhaberin (nen) ...... owner
der Kassierer (-) .... till operator

die Kassiererin (nen) ... till operator
der Kellner (-) .... waiter
die Kellnerin (nen) ...... waitress
der Koch (Köche) .... cook, chef
die Köchin (nen) .... cook, chef
der Kunde (n) *wk* .... customer
die Kundin (nen) .... customer
die Person (en) .... person

Allgemeines   General

die Auswahl .... choice
die Bedienung .... service, service charge
das Gericht (e) .... dish
der Geruch (Gerüche) .. smell
der Geschmack (Geschmäcke)
.... taste, flavour
das Hauptgericht (e)..... main dish
die britische Küche...... British food
die chinesische Küche . Chinese food
die deutsche Küche..... German food
die indische Küche ...... Indian food
das Kuvert (s) .... cover charge
die MwSt .... VAT
das Menü (s) .... set price menu
die Quittung (en) .... receipt
die Rechnung (en) .... bill
das Rezept (e) .... recipe
die Speisekarte (n)....... menu
die Spezialität (en) ...... speciality
der Stuhl (Stühle) .... chair
das Tablett (s) .... tray
das Tagesgericht (e)..... dish of the day
die Tageskarte (n)........ menu of the day
das Telefon (e)............. telephone
der Tisch (e) .... table
die Toiletten *pl* .... toilets
das Trinkgeld (er) .... tip (money)
die Weinkarte (n) .... wine list
der Zettel (-) .... chit

am Fenster.................. by the window

23

auf der Terrasse .... on the terrace
draußen .... outside
drinnen .... inside
(nicht) inbegriffen .... (not) included

Die Speisekarte   Menu
die Vorspeise (n) .... starter
das Hauptgericht (e) ..... main course
das Tagesgericht (e) ..... the day's "special"
der Nachtisch (e) .... dessert

Die Vorspeisen   Starters
der Aufschnitt .... mixed cold meats
die Hühnerbrühe .... chicken soup
die Leberwurst .... liver sausage
die Pastete (n) .... pâté
die kalte Platte .... mixed cold meats
die Suppe (n) .... soup
der Tomatensalat (e) .... tomato salad
die Wurst (Würste) ...... salami sausage

Das Hauptgericht   Main course
der Braten .... roast meat
das Brathähnchen (-) .... roast chicken
der Eintopf (Eintöpfe) .. casserole, stew
das Kalbschnitzel (-) .... veal escalope
das Kotelett (s) .... chop
das Omelett (s) .... omelette
die Pizza (s) .... pizza
der Rinderbraten .... roast beef
der Sauerbraten .... pickled roast beef
das Schweinekotelett (s)... pork chop
das Schweineschnitzel (-). pork escalope
das Steak (s) .... steak

Der Nachtisch   Dessert
der Apfelkuchen (-) ..... apple tart
der Apfelstrudel (-) ...... apple strudel
das Eis .... ice cream
der Joghurt (s) .... yoghurt
der Käsekuchen (-) ...... cheesecake
das Kompott .... stewed fruit
der Kuchen (-) .... gâteau

der Obstsalat .... fruit salad
der Pudding (-) .... cold milk dessert
die Schlagsahne .... whipped cream
das Schokoladeneis ...... chocolate ice cream
die Torte (n) .... flan
das Vanilleeis .... vanilla ice cream

Auf dem Tisch   On the table
das Besteck .... cutlery
die Flasche (n) .... bottle
die Gabel (n) .... fork
das Glas (Gläser) .... glass
die Kaffeekanne (n) ..... coffee pot
der Kaffeelöffel (n) ..... teaspoon
der Krug (Krüge) .... jug
der Löffel (-) .... spoon
das Messer (-) .... knife
der Pfeffer .... pepper (spice)
das Salz .... salt
die Schüssel (n) .... bowl
der Senf .... mustard
die Serviette (n) .... serviette, napkin
die Tasse (n) .... cup
der Teller (-) .... plate
die Tischdecke (n) .... tablecloth
die Untertasse (n) .... saucer

Im Café   At the café
Getränke   Drinks
der Apfelsaft .... apple juice
das Bier .... beer
die Cola .... Coca-cola®, cola
der Kaffee .... coffee
der Kakao .... cocoa
das Kännchen (-) .... individual pot
die Limonade (n) .... lemonade
das Mineralwasser .... mineral water
der Moselwein (e) .... Moselle wine
der Orangensaft (-säfte) orange juice
das Pils .... lager
der Rheinwein (e) .... Rhine wine
der Rotwein (e) .... red wine
der Saft (Säfte) .... fruit juice

der Schnaps .... spirits
die Schokolade .... chocolate
der Sekt .... German champagne
der Sprudel .... fizzy water; lemonade
der Tee .... tea
der Wein (e)............... wine
der Weißwein (e) .... white wine
der Zitronentee .... lemon tea

Der Imbiß   **A snack**
der Berliner.................. doughnut
die Bockwurst (-würste) .. frankfurter
die Bratwurst (-würste) fried sausage
die Chips *pl* .... crisps
die Currywurst (-würste) . curried sausage
das Eis .... ice cream
die Frikadelle (n) .... rissole
die Fritten *pl* .... chips
der Hamburger (-)........ beefburger
die Jägerwurst (-würste) .. sausage with
                           mushroom sauce
das Käsebrot (e) .... cheese sandwich
der Ketchup .... tomato ketchup
die Mayonnaise .... mayonnaise
die Pommes *pl* .... chips
die Pommes Frites *pl* ... chips
das Schinkenbrot (e) .... ham sandwich
der Senf .... mustard
die Waffel (n) .... waffle (edible)
die Zigeunerwurst (-würste)
                .... sausage with paprika sauce

Ausrufe   **Exclamations**
Das reicht! .... That is enough!
Fräulein! .... Waitress!
Guten Appetit!............ Enjoy your meal!
Herr Ober! .... Waiter!
Mahlzeit! .... Enjoy your meal!
(nein) danke................ (no) thank you!
Prost! .... Cheers!
Zahlen bitte! .... The bill, please

Nützliche Verben   **Useful verbs**
anbieten *irreg sep* .... to offer
bedienen † .... to serve
sich beklagen † .... to complain
bestellen † .... to order
bringen *irreg* .... to bring
einschenken *sep*.......... to pour
empfehlen *irreg* .... to recommend
essen *irreg* .... to eat
frühstücken.................. to have breakfast
Durst haben *irreg* .... to be thirsty
Hunger haben *irreg* ..... to be hungry
hassen......................... to hate
kosten † .... to cost
lieben .... to love
mögen *irreg* .... to like
nehmen *irreg* .... to take
probieren † .... to try
reichen .... to pass
reservieren † .... to reserve
schmecken.................. to taste
trinken *irreg* .... to drink
vorziehen *irreg sep* ...... to prefer
wählen......................... to choose
wollen *irreg* .... to want to
zu Abend essen *irreg* ... to have evening meal
zu Mittag essen *irreg* ... to have lunch

For festivals see page 44
For recipe words see page 55
For national and special foods see page 78
For lists of fruit, vegetables, fish, meat and
    general foodstuffs see page 53
For money and prices see pages 75, 56
For weights and measures see page 56

Redewendungen

Ich habe Hunger *I'm hungry*

Ich habe Durst *I'm thirsty*

Ein Kännchen Kaffee und einen Zitronentee, bitte *A pot of coffee and a lemon tea, please*

Zwei Glas Limonade und einen Orangensaft, bitte *Two glasses of lemonade and an orange juice, please*

Zwei Bier, bitte *Two beers, please*

Haben Sie einen Tisch für zwei? *Have you a table for two?*

Ich habe einen Tisch auf den Namen Smith reserviert *I've booked a table in the name of Smith*

Die Speisekarte, bitte *May I have the menu, please*

Können Sie mir bitte erklären, was „Spätzele" ist? *Please can you explain what "Spätzele" is?*

Ich möchte bestellen *I would like to order*

Ich nehme die Tageskarte *I'll have the menu of the day*

Als Vorspeise nehme ich die kalte Platte *For starter, I'll have the mixed cold meats*

Als Hauptgericht nehme ich Schweinebraten *I'll have roast pork for main course*

Ich esse nicht gern Zwiebeln *I don't like onions*

Als Nachtisch nehme ich ein gemischtes Eis *For dessert, I'll have a mixed ice cream*

Haben Sie Senf, bitte? *Have you got any mustard, please?*

Können Sie bitte dieses Glas austauschen? *Will you change this glass, please?*

Uns fehlt eine Gabel *We need another fork*

Zahlen, bitte! *May I have the bill, please?*

Ist die Bedienung inbegriffen? *Is service included?*

Wo sind die Toiletten, bitte? *Where are the toilets, please?*

Kann man von hier aus telefonieren? *May we phone from here?*

SELBST, FAMILIE, FREUNDE

Allgemeines	General
Die Anschrift	**Address**
die Adresse (n)	address
die Anschrift (en)	address
die Faxnummer (n)	fax number
die Hausnummer (n)	house number
die Postleitzahl (en)	postcode
die Stadt (Städte)	town
die Straße (n)	street, road
die Telefonnummer (n)	phone number
der Weg (e)	way
der Wohnort (e)	place of residence

Die Identität	**Identity**
der Ausweis (e)	identity card, ID
der Familienname (n) *wk* .	surname
Frau	Mrs, Ms
Fräulein	Miss
der Geburtsort (e)	place of birth
die Größe (n)	height, size
Herr (en)	Mr
die Identität (en)	identity
der Mädchenname (n) *wk*.	maiden name
der Name (n) *wk*	name
der Pass (Pässe)	passport
der Personalausweis (e)	identity card
der Spitzname (n) *wk* ...	nickname
die Unterschrift (en)	signature
der Vorname (n) *wk*	first name

Alter und Geburtstag	**Age and birthday**
das Alter	age, old age
das Datum (Daten)	date
die Geburt (en)	birth
das Geburtsdatum (-daten)	date of birth
der Geburtstag (e)	birthday
das Jahr (e)	year
der Monat (e)	month

Die Familie und Freunde
Family and friends

Die Kernfamilie	**Close family**
der Bruder (Brüder)	brother
das Einzelkind (er)	only child
die Eltern *pl*	parents
die Frau (en)	wife
der Halbbruder (-brüder) .	half brother
die Halbschwester (n) ..	half sister
der Mann (Männer)	husband
die Mutter (Mütter)	mother
die Mutti (s)	mummy
die Schwester (n)	sister
der Sohn (Söhne)	son
die Stiefmutter (-mütter)..	stepmother
der Stiefsohn (söhne) ...	stepson
die Stieftochter (-töchter)	stepdaughter
der Stiefvater (-väter) ..	stepfather
die Tochter (Töchter) ..	daughter
der Vater (Väter)	father
der Vati (s)	daddy

Andere Verwandte	**Other relatives**
der Cousin (s)	male cousin
die Cousine (n)	female cousin
der Enkel (-)	grandson
die Enkelin (nen)	granddaughter
das Enkelkind (er)	grandchild
die Großeltern *pl*	grandparents
die Großmutter (-mütter) .	grandmother
der Großvater (-väter)..	grandfather
die Kusine (n)	female cousin
der Neffe (n) *wk*	nephew
die Nichte (n)	niece
die Oma (s)	granny
der Onkel (-)	uncle
der Opa (s)	grandpa
der Schwager (Schwäger)	brother-in.law
die Schwägerin (nen)...	sister-in-law
die Schwiegermutter (-mütter)	
....	mother-in-law

der Schwiegersohn (-söhne).. son-in-law

die Schwiegertochter (-töchter)

.... daughter-in-law

der Schwiegervater (-väter)... father-in-law

die Tante (n)................ aunt

der Verwandte (n) ‡..... relative

der Vetter (-)............... male cousin

das Baby (s)................ baby

der Brieffreund (e)....... penfriend

die Brieffreundin (nen) penfriend

die Dame (n)............... lady

der Erwachsene (n) ‡... adult

die Frau (en)............... woman

der Freund (e).............. friend, boyfriend

die Freundin (nen)....... friend, girlfriend

der Bekannte (n) ‡...... friend

der Herr (en) *wk*........... gentleman

der Jugendliche (n) ‡... teenager, young person

der Junge (n) *wk*......... boy

das Kind (er)............... child

die Leute *pl*................ people

das Mädchen (-)........... girl

der Mann (Männer)...... man

der Nachbar (n) *wk*...... neighbour

die Nachbarin (nen)..... neighbour

der Verlobte (n) ‡........ fiancé

die Verlobte (n) ‡........ fiancée

der Alleinstehende (n) ‡... single man

die Alleinstehende (n) ‡... single woman

der Ausländer (-)......... foreigner

die Ausländerin (nen).. foreigner

der Fremde (n) ‡......... foreigner, stranger

die junge Generation ... the younger generation

der Geschiedene (n) ‡.. divorcee

der Junggeselle (n) *wk* . bachelor

die Senioren *pl* .... the older generation, senior citizens

die Witwe (n).............. widow

der Witwer (-)............. widower

die Zwillinge *pl* .... twins

Adjektive　　　　**Adjectives**

Adoptif‑..................... adopted

alt .... aged, elderly, old

älter........................... older, elder

Familien‑................... of the family

geschieden.................. divorced

getrennt...................... separated

jünger......................... younger

ledig........................... single, unmarried

unverheiratet.............. single, unmarried

verheiratet.................. married

verlobt........................ engaged

verwaist...................... orphaned

verwitwet................... widowed

anglikanisch............... anglican

atheistisch.................. atheist

christlich.................... Christian

evangelisch................. Protestant

hindu.......................... Hindu

jüdisch........................ Jewish

katholisch................... Catholic

mohammedanisch........ Muslim

sikhisch...................... Sikh

ohne Konfession.......... of no religion

Das Aussehen　　　**Appearance**

der Bart (Bärte).......... beard

die Brille (n)............... pair of glasses

der Ehering (e)........... wedding ring

das Gewicht................ weight

die Größe (n).............. size

der Oberlippenbart (-bärte)........ moustache

der Pferdeschwanz (-schwänze).. pony tail

der Pony (s).............,....... fringe

die Taille (n) .... size, waist

der Zopf (Zöpfe) .... plait

alt .... old

blass........................... pale

blond.......................... blonde

dick............................ fat

dünn........................... thin

frisiert.........................curly (frizzy)
gebräunt ....tanned
glatt............................straight (hair)
groß............................big, tall
hässlich.......................ugly
hübsch.........................pretty
jung............................young
klein...........................small
kurz............................short
lang............................long
lockig..........................curly (wavy)
mittelgroß....................of average height
rothaarig......................red-haired
schlank........................slim
schön..........................handsome, beautiful
schwarz.......................black
solid............................stocky, sturdy
stark ....strong
untersetzt.....................stocky
weiß............................white

Ich bin ... groß   I am ... tall
Ich bin 1m 45 groß ......I am 4ft 9in
Ich bin 1m 52 groß ......I am 5 ft
Ich bin 1m 60 groß ......I am 5ft 3in
Ich bin 1m 68 groß ......I am 5ft 6in
Ich bin 1m 75 groß ......I am 5ft 9in
Ich bin 1m 83 groß ......I am 6ft

Ich wiege   I weigh
Ich wiege 38 Kilo ....I weigh 6 stone
Ich wiege 44 Kilo ....I weigh 7 stone
Ich wiege 51 Kilo ....I weigh 8 stone
Ich wiege 57 Kilo ....I weigh 9 stone
Ich wiege 63 Kilo ....I weigh 10 stone
Ich wiege 70 Kilo ....I weigh 11 stone
Ich wiege 76 Kilo ....I weigh 12 stone

Farben   Colours
blau ....blue
braun ....brown
dunkelblau...................dark blue
gelb ....yellow

grau.............................grey
grün.............................green
hellblau ....light blue
hellbraun ....light brown, chestnut
lila *inv* ....mauve
marineblau ....navy blue
orange ....orange
purpur *inv*....................purple
rosa *inv*.......................pink
rot ....red
schwarz.......................black
weiß............................white

Der Charakter   Character
die Arroganz ....arrogance
der Charme..................charm
die Eifersucht..............jealousy
die Faulheit ....laziness
die Freundschaft (en)... friendship
das Gefühl (e) ....feeling
die Großzügigkeit........ generosity
die Hoffnung (en)........hope
die Intelligenz ....intelligence
die Freundlichkeit ....kindness
die Liebe (n)...............love
das Selbstbewusstsein .. confidence
die Selbstsucht ....selfishness
der Sinn für Humor ..... sense of humour
die Sorge (n) ....care, worry
der Stolz.....................pride
die Vorstellungskraft... imagination
der Witz (e) ....joke

aktiv ....active
böse............................angry; naughty; nasty
dumm.........................stupid
faul.............................lazy, idle
fleißig.........................hard-working
freundlich...................friendly
fröhlich ....happy, cheerful, merry
glücklich ....happy, pleased
intelligent ....intelligent

komisch	funny, amusing		talentiert	gifted
lustig	amusing		unbeholfen	clumsy
nett	kind		ungezogen	rude (very)
sportlich	sporty, athletic		verliebt (in + acc)	in love (with)
sympathisch	nice		verwöhnt	spoilt (child)
traurig	sad		wütend	furious
unglücklich	unhappy, unfortunate		zornig	angry
verrückt	mad			
wichtig	important			
wunderbar	great, fantastic			
zufrieden	content			

Die Staatsangehörigkeit   Nationality

britisch	British
englisch	English
europäisch	European
indisch	Indian
irisch	Irish
pakistanisch	Pakistani
schottisch	Scottish
walisisch	Welsh
westindisch	West Indian

angenehm	pleasant
arm	poor
egoistisch	selfish
ekelhaft	disgusting
enttäuscht	disappointed
ernst	serious
höflich	polite
nervös	nervous
niedlich	cute
ruhig	calm
schüchtern	shy
stolz	proud
unangenehm	unpleasant
unausstehlich	unbearable
unhöflich	impolite

For other nationalities see page 87

Die Haustiere   Pets

der Goldfisch (e)	goldfish
der Hamster (-)	hamster
das Haustier (e)	pet
der Hund (e)	dog
die Hündin (nen)	bitch
der junge Hund	puppy
das Kaninchen (-)	rabbit
der Kater (-)	tomcat
das Kätzchen (-)	kitten
die Katze (n)	cat
die Maus (Mäuse)	mouse
das Meerschweinchen (-)	guinea pig
das Pferd (e)	horse
die Schildkröte (n)	tortoise
der Vogel (Vögel)	bird
der Wellensittich (e)	budgerigar
die Wüstenspringmaus (-mäuse)	gerbil

ängstlich	frightened, anxious
artig	well-behaved
charmant	charming
deprimiert	depressed
ehrlich	honest
eifersüchtig	jealous
geistesabwesend	absent-minded
klug	clever
mürrisch	sullen
schlau	clever, cunning, wily
seltsam	odd, strange
sparsam	thrifty, careful with money
still	quiet
stur	obstinate

Wie ist es?   What it it like?

aggressiv	aggressive
alt	old

bissig .... likely to bite
gehorsam .... obedient
groß .... big
jung .... young
klein .... small
lieb .... nice, well-behaved
spielerisch.................. playful (puppy, kitten)
unartig .... naughty

Nützliche Verben   Useful verbs
Angst haben *irreg* .... to be afraid
aussehen *irreg sep* .... to look (like)
beschreiben *irreg* .... to describe
buchstabieren † .... to spell
danken (+ dat) .... to thank
erkennen *irreg* .... to recognise
erscheinen *irreg* .... to appear
finden *irreg* .... to find
geboren sein* *irreg* ...... to be born
guter Laune sein* *irreg* to be in a good mood
heiraten † .... to marry

heißen *irreg* .... to be called
kennen lernen *sep* .... to get to know
küssen .... to kiss
lieben .... to like, love
nennen *irreg* .... to name
plaudern .... to chatter
scheinen *irreg* .... to seem
schreiben *irreg* .... to write
schlechter Laune sein* *irreg*
.... to be in a bad mood
sein* *irreg* .... to be
tragen *irreg* .... to wear; to carry
unterschreiben *irreg insep* to sign
wiegen *irreg* .... to weigh
wohnen....................... to live, reside

For festivals and celebrations see page 44
For jobs see page 70
For pocket money see page 37
For Saturday jobs see page 32
For hobbies and interests see page 32

Redewendungen

Ich heiße David. Ich bin sechzehn Jahre alt. Ich wohne in London *My name is David. I am 16.*
   I live in London
Ich habe am neunzehnten Mai Geburtstag *My birthday is May 19th*
Ich bin neunzehnhundertvierundachtzig geboren *I was born in 1984*
Ich komme aus Edinburg *I come from Edinburgh*
Ich bin in York geboren *I was born in York*
Ich bin Engländer/Ire/Schotte/Waliser *I am English/Irish/Scottish/Welsh (and male)*
Ich bin Engländerin/Irin/Schottin/Waliserin *I am English/Irish/Scottish/Welsh (and female)*
Ich habe schwarze Haare und braune Augen *I have black hair and brown eyes*
Er hat einen grauen Bart *He has a grey beard*
Ich bin Einzelkind *I am an only child*
Ich habe einen Bruder und zwei Schwestern *I have one brother and two sisters*
David ist älter als Sue *David is older than Sue*
Mein Vater ist Mechaniker, meine Mutter ist Krankenschwester *My father is a mechanic, my*
   mother is a nurse
Meine Eltern sind geschieden *My parents are divorced*
Ich verstehe mich gut mit meinem Bruder *I get on well with my brother*
Meine Schwester ist sehr sportlich *My sister is very keen on sport*
Ich habe eine Katze und einen Hund *I have a cat and a dog*
Mein Hund ist groß und braun *My dog is big and brown*

FREIZEIT UND WOCHENENDE

Allgemeines — General

der Abend (e)............... evening
das Abonnement (s) ..... subscription, season ticket
die Atmosphäre (n)...... atmosphere
die Ferien *pl* .... holidays
die Freizeit .... free time
das Hobby (s).............. hobby
die Party (s)................. party
die Unterhaltung.......... entertainment
der Wettbewerb (e)...... competition
das Wochenende (n)..... weekend
der Zeitvertreib (e)....... pastime

Leute — People

der Heranwachsende (n) ‡ .... adolescent
die Jugend .... youth, young people
die Mannschaft (en)..... team
der Meister (-) .... champion
die Meisterin (-) .... champion
das Mitglied (er) .... member
der Sänger (-) .... singer
die Sängerin (nen) .... singer
der Schauspieler (-)...... actor
die Schauspielerin (nen) .. actress
der Schiedsrichter (-) ... referee
der Spieler (-) .... player
die Spielerin (nen) .... player
der Star (s).................. film star
der Teenager (-).......... teenager
die Teenagerin (nen).... teenager

Samstagsjobs — Saturday jobs

die Arbeit (en) .... work
das Babysitten............. baby sitting
der Fußballklub (s) ...... football club
der Kassierer (-).......... till operator
die Kassiererin (nen) ... till operator
der Markt (Märkte) ...... market
der Morgen (-) .... morning

der Nachmittag (e)....... afternoon
der Supermarkt (-märkte) .supermarket
die Tankstelle (n) .... filling station
der Tennisklub (s) .... tennis club
der Verkäufer (-) .... sales assistant
die Verkäuferin (nen) .. sales assistant

Nützliche Verben — Useful verbs

arbeiten † .... to work
austragen *irreg sep* ..... to deliver (newspapers)
liefern........................ to deliver
putzen .... to clean
verdienen †.................. to earn money
verkaufen † .... to sell

Zu Hause helfen — Helping at home

Am Wochenende muss ich ...
.... At the weekend, I have to ...
den Tisch abräumen *sep* ...to clear the table
im Garten arbeiten †.... ....to work in the garden
auf Kinder aufpassen *sep*..to baby sit
mein Zimmer aufräumen *sep* .to tidy my room
bügeln .... to iron
den Tisch decken......... to set the table
fegen .... to sweep
den Hund spazieren führen *sep*
.... to walk the dog
die Katze füttern.......... to feed the cat
einkaufen gehen* *irreg* to do the shopping
Hausarbeit machen...... to do housework
mein Bett machen........ to make my bed
den Rasen mähen......... to mow the lawn
putzen .... to clean
spülen......................... to wash up
Staub wischen .... to dust
das Auto waschen *irreg* to wash the car

Zu Hause bleiben — Staying at home

Was machst du?   **What do you do?**
das Basteln .... model-making
die Briefmarke (n)....... stamp

das Damenspiel............ draughts
der Film (e)................. film
der Fotoapparat (e) ...... camera
das Fotografieren......... photography
das Gesellschaftsspiel (e) . board game
die Illustrierte (n) ‡..... magazine
die Karten *pl*............... cards
das Kochen................. cooking
das Kreuzworträtsel (-) crossword
der Kriminalroman (e) . detective story
die Lektüre................. reading
das Malen................... painting
die Musik................... music
das Nähen................... sewing
das Poster (-)............... poster
der Roman (e).............. novel
die Sammlung (en) ...... collection
das Schach................. chess
der Science-Fiction-Roman (e)
.... sci-fi story
das Zeichnen............... drawing
die Zeitschrift (en)....... magazine

Informatik   **IT**
der Bildschirm (e)........ screen, monitor
das Byte .... byte
der CD ROM (s) .... CD ROM
der Chip (s)................. chip
der Computer (-)......... computer
die Computermusik ..... computer music
das Computerspiel (e) .. computer game
die Datei (en).............. data-base, file
der Diskmanager (-)..... disk manager
der Diskdrive (s) .... disk drive
die Diskette (n)........... disk
der Drucker (-)............ printer
die Festplatte (n)......... hard disk
der Joystick (s)............ joystick
das Leben (-)............... life
der Leuchtstift (e) .... light pen
die Maus (Mäuse) .... mouse
das Menü (s) .... menu
die Tastatur (en) .... keyboard

die Textverarbeitung ... word processing
das Videospiel (e) .... video game
aufmachen *sep*............ to open
bearbeiten †................ to edit
drucken .... to print
formatieren †............... to format
laden *irreg*................. to load
speichern.................... to save

Die Musik   **Music**
die Band (s)................ group
die Blockflöte (n) .... recorder
die CD (s)................... CD
der Chor (Chöre) .... choir
der Flügel (-) .... grand piano
die Geige (n) .... violin
die Gitarre (n) .... guitar
der Hit (s) .... hit song (in English)
das Instrument (e) .... instrument
die Kassette (n) .... cassette
die Klarinette (n) .... clarinet
das Klavier (e) .... piano (upright)
das Lied (er) .... song
das Orchester (-) .... orchestra, band
die Posaune (n)........... trombone
die Querflöte (n)......... flute
der Schlager (-)........... hit song (in German)
das Schlagzeug .... drum kit
die Trompete (n) .... trumpet
der Walkman® (Walkmen).. personal stereo

Wo gehst du hin?   **Where do you go?**
der Abend (e) .... evening
der Ausflug (Ausflüge) outing
die Ausstellung (en) .... exhibition
der Ball (Bälle)........... ball
die Disco (s) .... disco
die Eisbahn (en) .... ice rink
das Freibad (-bäder)..... open air swimming
              pool
die Führung (en).......... guided tour
die Halle (n) .... hall (public, sport)
das Hallenbad (-bäder). indoor swimming pool

der Jugendklub (s) .... youth club
die Kegelbahn (en) ...... bowling alley
das Kino (s) .... cinema
das Konzert (e) .... concert
die Kunstgalerie (n) ..... gallery
der Nachtklub (s) .... night club
die Party (s) .... party (celebration)
das Schwimmbad (-bäder) .... swimming pool
der Sportplatz (-plätze) sports ground
das Sportzentrum (-zentren) .. sports centre
das Stadion (Stadien) ... stadium
der Tanz (Tänze) .... dance
das Theater .... theatre
der Verein (e) .... club, society
die Vorlesung (en) .... lecture
der Zirkus (se) .... circus
der Zoo (s) .... zoo

Der Sport   Sport

Allgemeines   **General**
die Mannschaft (en) ..... team
der Meister (-) .... champion
die Meisterin (nen) ...... champion
die Meisterschaft (en) .. championship
das Spiel (e) .... match, game
der Spieler (-) .... player
die Spielerin (nen) .... player
das Tor (e) .... goal
das Tournier (e) .... tournament
das Unentschieden .... draw
der Wettbewerb (e) ...... competition, contest

Welchen Sport treibst du gern?
                Which sport do you like?
das Angeln .... fishing
der Basketball .... basketball
der Fußball .... football
das Golf .... golf
die Gymnastik .... gymnastics
das Hockey .... hockey
das Jogging .... jogging
der Korbball .... netball
das Kricket .... cricket

die Leichtathletik .... athletics
das Radfahren .... cycling
das Reiten .... horse riding
das Rugby .... rugby
das Schwimmen .... swimming
das Tennis .... tennis
das Tischtennis .... table tennis
der Volleyball .... volleyball

der Boxsport .... boxing
das Darts .... darts
das Drachenfliegen ...... hang gliding
der Handball .... handball
der Hochsprung .... high jump
das Judo .... judo
die Kampfsportarten *pl* martial arts
das Kegeln .... bowling
das Rollschuhlaufen ..... roller skating
das Schlittschuhlaufen . ice skating
das Segeln .... sailing
das Skilaufen .... ski-ing
das Snooker .... snooker
der Wassersport .... water sports
der Weitsprung .... long jump
das Windsurfen .... sail boarding
der Wintersport .... winter sports

Die Sportausrüstung Sports equipment
die Angelrute (n) .... fishing rod
der Badeanzug (-züge) . swimsuit
die Badehose (n) .... bathing trunks
der Ball (Bälle) .... ball
der Fußball (-bälle) ...... football
der Fußballschuh (e) .... football boot
der Hockeyschläger (-) hockey stick
der Kricketschläger (-). cricket bat
das Mountainbike (s) ... mountain bike
die Reitkappe (n) .... riding hat
der Ski (s) .... ski
das Surfbrett (er) .... surfboard, sailboard
der Tennisschläger (-).. tennis racket
der Turnschuh (e) .... trainer (shoe)

Wie war es?	**What was it like?**
amüsant	funny
andere..........................	other
angenehm	pleasant
astrein *coll*	great, super
aufregend.....................	exciting
ausgezeichnet	excellent
eindrucksvoll	impressive
einmalig	great, brilliant
furchtbar......................	awful
nicht gestattet	not allowed
gut	good
langweilig....................	boring
laut	noisy
lustig	amusing, fun
nett	nice
nutzlos........................	useless
prima...........................	great
nicht schlecht..............	not bad
schrecklich	awful
sportlich	sporty, keen on sport
super...........................	super
wunderbar	marvellous

Eintrittskarten kaufen   Buying tickets
der Erwachsene (n) ‡... adult
der Eintritt .... entrance (cost)
die Eintrittskarte (n) .... ticket
die Ermäßigung (en).... reduced rate
die Gruppe (n) .... group
das Kind (er)............... child
der Platz (Plätze) .... seat; ground, pitch
der Preis (e) .... cost, price
die Schülerermäßigung (en)
.... reduction for children
der Student (en) *wk* ...... student
die Studentenermäßigung (en)
.... student rate
der Schüler (-) .... school student
der Tarif .... cost

Öffnungszeiten   Opening times
am Abend.................... in the evening
an Feiertagen .... on bank holidays

am Morgen.................. in the morning
am Nachmittag .... in the afternoon
um ein Uhr .... at one o'clock

eine halbe Stunde .... half an hour
die Stunde (n).............. hour, sixty minutes

geschlossen .... closed
geöffnet...................... open

von (+ dat) .... from
bis (+ acc) .... until

In die Stadt gehen Going into town
mit dem Auto .... by car
mit der Bahn............... by train
mit dem Bus .... by bus
zu Fuß .... on foot
mit dem Rad............... on a bicycle
mit der Straßenbahn .... by tram
mit dem Taxi.............. by taxi
mit der U-Bahn .... on the underground
mit dem Wagen .... by car
mit dem Zug............... by train

der Bahnhof (-höfe) ..... station
der Busbahnhof (-höfe) bus station
die Bushaltestelle (n)... bus stop
die Buslinie (n)........... bus route
die einfache Fahrkarte . single ticket
der Fahrkartenautomat (en) *wk*
.... ticket machine
der Fahrkartenschalter (-) ticket office
der Fahrplan (-pläne) ... timetable
die Hauptverkehrszeit (en) rush hour
die Rückfahrkarte (n) .. return ticket
die Straßenbahnhaltestelle (n).. tram stop
die Straßenbahnlinie (n) .... tram line
die U-Bahnstation (en) underground station
die Verbindung (en) .... connection
das Verkehrsamt (-ämter) information office

Adjektive   Adjectives
direkt.......................... direct, through
erst .... first

erster Klasse .... first class

gültig .... valid

letzt .... last

nächst .... next

pflicht *inv* .... compulsory

zweit .... second

zweiter Klasse .... second class

Wann? **When?**

in zehn Minuten .... in ten minutes

in einer Viertelstunde .. in a quarter of an hour

in einer halben Stunde . in half an hour

in einer Dreiviertelstunde in three quarters of
an hour

in einer Stunde .... in an hour

gewöhnlich .... usually

immer .... always

lange .... for a long time

noch .... still

normalerweise .... usually

am Wochenende .... at the weekend

Nützliche Verben **Useful verbs**

ausgehen* *irreg sep* ..... to go out

beginnen *irreg* .... to begin

besuchen † .... to go and see

bezahlen † .... to pay (for)

bleiben* *irreg* .... to stay

dauern .... to last

fahren* *irreg* .... to go

finden *irreg* .... to find

gehen* *irreg* .... to go

hören .... to listen (to)

kaufen .... to buy

kosten † .... to cost

lesen *irreg* .... to read

sammeln .... to collect (things)

schließen *irreg* .... to close

schwimmen (*) *irreg* ... to swim

sein* *irreg* .... to be

spazieren gehen* *irreg* . to go for a walk

tanzen .... to dance

verlassen *irreg* .... to leave

enden † .... to finish

in die Stadt gehen* *irreg* ..to go to town

gewinnen *irreg* .... to win

sich interessieren für (+ acc) †
.... to be interested in

laufen* *irreg* .... to run

einen Einkaufsbummel machen
.... to go round the shops

Fotos machen .... to take photos

einen Schaufensterbummel machen
.... to go window shopping

Rad fahren* *irreg sep* .. to cycle

reiten* *irreg* .... to go horse riding

einen Platz reservieren † ...to book a seat

Karten spielen .... to play cards

Sport treiben *irreg* .... to do sport

wandern* .... to hike, go for a long
walk

zurückgehen* *irreg sep* to go back

zurückkommen* *irreg sep* to come back

zusehen *irreg sep* .... to watch

angeln gehen* *irreg* ..... to go fishing

aufhören *sep* .... to stop (doing sthg)

sich ausruhen *sep* .... to rest

basteln .... to do odd jobs/DIY

sich befinden *irreg* .... to be (situated)

ein Schloss besuchen † to look round a stately
home/castle

einen Film drehen .... to make a film

sich entspannen † .... to relax

entwerten † .... to date-stamp ticket

Rollschuh fahren* *irreg* ....to roller-skate

Ski fahren* *irreg* .... to ski

nach Hause kommen* *irreg*
.... to come back home

Schlittschuh laufen* *irreg* to skate

eine Radfahrt machen.. to go cycling

malen .... to paint

modellieren † .... to make models

ein Tor schießen *irreg* . to score a goal

segeln .... to go sailing
im Chor singen *irreg*.... to sing in the choir
Klavier spielen............. to play the piano
Schlagzeug spielen ...... to play the drums
Schlange stehen *irreg* .. to queue
stempeln .... to stamp
das Haus verlassen *irreg* .. to leave the house
verlieren *irreg*.............. to lose
verteidigen †................ to defend
windsurfen................... to windsurf
zeichnen † .... to draw

zum Gottesdienst gehen* *irreg*
.... to go to (protestant) church
zur Messe gehen* *irreg* .... to go to mass
zur Moschee gehen* *irreg* to go to the mosque
zur Synagoge gehen* *irreg*
.... to go to the synagogue

For seaside holidays see page 79
For winter sports see page 79
For outings see page 80
For special occasions and festivals see page 44

Redewendungen

Ich spiele Fußball *I play football*
Ich spiele Geige *I play the violin*
Ich gehe gern angeln *I like going fishing*
Wir haben das Fußballspiel gewonnen *We won the football match*
Ich interessiere mich für Musik *I am interested in music*
Ich kann Seifenopern nicht ausstehen *I hate soaps*
Meine Lieblingslektüre ist Science-Fiction *My favourite kind of book is science fiction*

TASCHENGELD

Allgemeines   General

der Geldschein (e)........ bank note
das Kleingeld .... change
die Münze (n) .... coin
das Pfund .... pound

arm............................ poor, badly-off
reich .... rich
teuer .... expensive
viel .... a lot
wohlhabend .... well-off

pro Monat................... per month
pro Woche.................. each week

Wofür gibst du dein Geld aus?
Spending money

die CD (s)................... CD
die Eintrittskarte (n) .... ticket (entertainment)
die Fahrkarte (n)......... ticket (travel)
die Kassette (n) .... cassette
die Kleidung.............. clothes
der Schuh (e) .... shoe
der Sportschuh (e) .... trainer (shoe)
das Videospiel (e) .... video game
der Walkman® (Walkmen).. personal stereo
die Zeitschrift (en)....... magazine
die Zigarette (n) .... cigarette

Sparen   Saving money

der Computer (-) .... computer

die Ferien *pl* .... holidays

das Geschenk (e) .... present

das Mountainbike (s) ... mountain bike

Nützliche Verben   Useful verbs

ausgeben *irreg sep* .... to spend

zu viel ausgeben *irreg sep*

.... to spend too much money

brauchen .... to need

kaufen .... to buy

kosten † .... to cost

leihen *irreg* .... to borrow, lend

knapp bei Kasse sein* *irreg* ...to be short of money

pleite sein* *irreg* .... to be broke

sparen .... to save

in den roten Zahlen stehen *irreg*

.... to be in the red

eine Stelle suchen .... to look for a job

For other money words see page 75

Redewendungen

Ich verdiene ... Mark pro Stunde *I earn ... marks an hour*

Ich arbeite samstags *I work on Saturdays*

Ich fange um acht Uhr morgens an und ich arbeite bis fünf Uhr nachmittags *I start at eight in the morning and finish at five in the afternoon*

Ich spare für einen Computer *I am saving up to buy a computer*

Ich habe alles ausgegeben *I've spent everything*

Ich bin pleite *I'm broke*

ZWISCHENMENSCHLICHE KONTAKTE

Begrüßungen   Exchanging greetings

Guten Morgen! .... Good Morning
Guten Tag! .... Good Afternoon
Guten Abend! .... Good Evening
Hallo! .... Hi!
Auf Wiedersehen! .... Goodbye
Bis bald! .... See you soon
Bis später! .... See you later
Bis morgen! .... See you tomorrow

Wie geht's? .... How are you?
Gut, danke .... Very well, thank you
Mittelmäßig .... So-so
Darf ich Udo vorstellen?
.... May I introduce Udo?
Angenehm .... Pleased to meet you
Herzlich willkommen!. Welcome!

Herein! .... Come in
Nehmen Sie Platz! .... Sit down
Bitte .... Please
Danke .... Thank you
Entschuldigen Sie! .... Excuse me

Füllsel   Fillers

Ja, natürlich .... Yes, of course
Abgemacht .... Agreed
Das ist freundlich........ That's nice
Mit Vergnügen .... With pleasure
Ich glaube ja .... I think so
Ich glaube nicht .... I don't think so
Vermutlich .... I suppose so
Ich nehme an .... I suppose so
Vielleicht .... Perhaps
Das ist mir egal........... I don't mind
Schade! .... What a shame!

Entschuldigungen Apologising

Verzeihung! .... Sorry
Es tut mir Leid........... I am sorry

Ich habe es nicht extra gemacht
.... I didn't do it on purpose

Kein Problem .... No problem
Das macht nichts .... It doesn't matter
Gern geschehen .... Don't mention it
Machen Sie sich keine Sorgen darüber!
.... Don't worry

Glückwünsche   Best wishes

Herzlichen Glückwunsch zum Geburtstag!
.... Happy Birthday!
Ein glückliches neues Jahr!
.... Happy New Year!
Hals- und Beinbruch! .. Good luck!
Einen schönen Tag noch! .Have a nice day!
Fröhliche Weihnachten! ...Happy Christmas!
Frohe Ostern! .... Happy Easter!

Meinungen   Opinions

Ich mag .... I like ...
Ich mag nicht .... I don't like ...
Ich liebe .... I love ...
Ich hasse .... I hate ...
Ich kann ... nicht ausstehen.. I can't stand ...

Es kommt darauf an .... It depends
Ich esse lieber............. I prefer eating ...
Ich höre lieber............ I prefer listening to ...
Ich lerne lieber .... I prefer learning ...
Ich spiele lieber .... I prefer playing ...

Es ist beschissen *coll* ... It's lousy
Es ist ekelhaft............. It's disgusting
Es ist furchtbar .... It's awful
Es ist interessant......... It's interesting
Es ist langweilig......... It's boring
Es ist super................. It's superb
Es schmeckt .... It's delicious

freundlich.................. kind
nett............................ nice

schrecklich .... awful
schwierig .... difficult

schlecht in .... poor at
gut in .... good at
hoffnungslos in .... useless at

Fragen   Questions

Wann? .... When?
Warum? .... Why?
Was? .... What?
Welche? .... Which?
Wer? .... Who?
Wie? .... How?
Wie ist ...? .... What is ... like?
Wie viele? .... How many?
Wie viel? .... How much?

Darf ich ...? .... May I ...? Can I ...?
Darf man ...? .... Can we ...? Can you ...?
Könnte ich ...? .... Could I ...?

Probleme der Jugendlichen
Teenage problems

Leute   **People**
die Eltern *pl* .... parents
der Freund (e) .... friend, boyfriend
die Freundin (nen) .... friend, girlfriend
der Jugendliche (n) ‡ ... teenager
der Kamerad (en) *wk*.... friend, mate
die Kameradin (nen).... friend, mate
der Lehrer (-) .... teacher
die Lehrerin (nen)........ teacher

die Arbeit .... work
die Arbeitslosigkeit ..... unemployment
die Ausbildung (en) ..... training (job)
der Dieb (e) .... thief
die Diebin (nen) .... thief
der Elterndruck........... parental pressure
das Fach (Fächer)........ school subject
der Geldmangel .... lack of money

der Generationsunterschied (e)
.... generation gap
der Job (s) .... job (part-time)
der Ladendieb (e) .... shoplifter
der Ladendiebstahl ...... shop lifting
die Lehrstelle (n) .... apprenticeship
die Leserbriefe *pl* .... agony column
die Lüge (n) .... lie
die Mode (n) .... fashion
das Nachsitzen............ detention
der Pickel (-) .... spot, zit
die Popmusik .... pop music
die Prüfung (en) .... examinations
die tägliche Routine ..... daily routine
die Schularbeit .... school work
der Schulstress .... stress at school
die Schuluniform .... school uniform
das Schwänzen .... truancy, skiving
der Stress.................... stress

das Aids .... AIDS
die Droge (n)............... drug
die Einstellung (en) ...... attitude
der Einwanderer (-) ...... immigrant
die Farbe (n) .... colour
das Frauenhaus (häuser) ... women's refuge
die Gewalttätigkeit .... violence
die Hautfarbe (n)......... skin colour
der Missbrauch............ abuse
der Obdachlose (n) ‡ .... homeless person
der Rassismus.............. racism
der Rowdy (s)............... hooligan
die Scheidung (en) .... divorce
das Schikanieren.......... bullying
der Transportmangel .... lack of transport
der Überfall (Überfälle) robbery, mugging
der Vandalismus........... vandalism
das Zuhause (n) .... home

Adjektive   **Adjectives**
alkoholisch.................. alcoholic
artig .... well-behaved
begabt .... gifted

benachteiligt .... disadvantaged
faul .... lazy
gelangweilt .... bored
gestresst .... stressed out
gut informiert .... well-informed
intelligent .... intelligent
langweilig .... boring
offensichtlich .... glaring, obvious
pflicht *inv* .... compulsory
priviligiert .... privileged
schlecht informiert .... ill-informed
schwach (in) .... no good (at)
verwöhnt .... spoilt (child)
weit außerhalb der Stadt
.... a long way out of town

Bemerkungen   Expressions
Es geht mir auf die Nerven
.... It gets on my nerves
Das macht müde .... It makes me tired
Das ärgert mich .... It irritates me/
It annoys me
Es langweilt mich .... It bores me

Nützliche Verben   Useful verbs
aufräumen *sep* .... to tidy up
spät aufstehen* *irreg sep* . to get up late
erlauben † .... to allow
schwer finden *irreg* ...... to find something
difficult
früh ins Bett gehen* *irreg* ....to go to bed early

spät ins Bett gehen* *irreg* .to go to bed late
Spaß haben *irreg* .... to have fun
im Haushalt helfen *irreg*
.... to help in the house
müssen *irreg* .... to have to
schwänzen.................. to skive off school
sich streiten *irreg* .... to fight, dispute
spülen........................ to do the washing up
Geld verdienen † .... to earn money
vergessen *irreg*........... to forget
verlieren *irreg* .... to lose
verstehen *irreg* .... to understand
sich gut verstehen *irreg* mit (+ dat)
.... to get on well with
werden* *irreg*.............. to become
wiederholen *insep* .... to revise

akzeptieren † .... to accept
erröten † .... to blush
lügen........................ to lie
die Wahrheit sagen...... to tell the truth
stehlen *irreg* .... to steal
Kritik üben................. to criticise
die Wahrheit verbergen *irreg*
.... to hide the truth
von der Schule verweisen *irreg*
.... to expel

For leisure time and activities see page 32
For café and restaurant see page 23
For TV, radio, music, etc see page 16

Redewendungen und Fragen

Verstehst du dich gut mit deinen Eltern/mit deiner Mutter/mit deinem Vater/mit deinem
Bruder/mit deiner Schwester? *Do you get on well with your parents/mother/
father/brother/sister?*

Hast du Schwierigkeiten in der Schule? *Have you any problems at school?*

Darfst du in der Woche/am Wochenende mit deinen Freunden/mit deinen Freundinnen ausgehen?
Are you allowed to go out with your friends during the week/at weekends?

Worüber streitet man bei dir zu Hause? *What do you argue about at home?*

Was ärgert dich? *What annoys you?*

Was mich ärgert ist ... *What annoys me is ...*

AUSGEHEN

Wo gehen wir hin?
Where shall we go?

das Café (s)................. café
die Disco (s)............... disco
die Eisbahn (en) .... ice rink
das Eiscafé (s)............. ice cream parlour
das Freibad (-bäder)..... open air swimming pool
das Geschäft (e) .... shop
das Hallenbad (-bäder). indoor swimming pool
das Kino (s)................ cinema
der Laden (Läden) .... shop
der Nachtklub (s)......... nightclub
der Park (s)................. park
die Party (s)................ party (celebration)
das Spiel (e)................ match
das Sportzentrum (-zentren). sports centre
das Theater .... theatre

Annehmen   Accepting

Abgemacht .... OK, agreed
Danke........................ Thank you
Es kommt darauf an..... It depends
gern........................... with pleasure, gladly
gut .... good
Ja .... Yes
Klasse *inv*.................. super
natürlich .... of course
nett............................ nice, kind
in Ordnung .... OK
sicher......................... certainly

Ablehnen   Refusing

Es geht nicht, weil ...... It's impossible,
                              because ...
Es tut mir Leid, aber ... Sorry, but ...
Leider ... . I'm afraid ...
Ich kann nicht............. I can't
Ich bin verabredet........ I'm not free

nein, danke .... no thank you

leider.......................... unfortunately

Wann treffen wir uns?
When shall we meet?

um halb acht............... at 7.30
bald........................... soon
heute Abend............... this evening
heute Nachmittag .... this afternoon
in zwei Stunden.......... in two hours
morgen...................... tomorrow
übermorgen................ the day after tomorrow
nächste Woche .... next week
nächsten Montag .... next Monday
am Wochenende......... at the weekend

Wo treffen wir uns?
Where shall we meet?

an der Bushaltestelle.... at the bus stop
im Café .... in the café
vor dem Kino .... in front of the cinema
am Bahnhof................ at the station
am Busbahnhof .... at the bus station
im Restaurant .... at the restaurant

in (+ dat) .... in
vor (+ dat) .... in front of
hinter (+ dat) .... behind
rechts von (+ dat) .... to the right of
links von (+ dat) .... to the left of
gegenüber (+ dat) .... opposite

Nützliche Verben   Useful verbs

ablehnen *sep*............... to refuse
ankommen* *irreg sep*.. to arrive
annehmen *irreg sep* ..... to accept
ausgehen* *irreg sep*..... to go out
begleiten †................. to accompany, go with
besuchen † .... to go and see
danken (+ dat) .... to thank
einladen *irreg sep* .... to invite

entscheiden *irreg* .... to decide
fragen .... to ask
kommen* *irreg* .... to come
können *irreg* .... to be able to, can
kosten † .... to cost
meinen........................ to think
man muss *irreg* .... we must, you have to
sehen *irreg*.................. to see
sich verabreden † .... to arrange to meet
stattfinden *irreg sep* ..... to take place
tanzen .... to dance
treffen *irreg* .... to meet
vergessen *irreg* .... to forget
vorschlagen *irreg sep*... to suggest
warten auf † (+ acc)..... to wait for
wissen *irreg* .... to know (a fact)
wollen *irreg* .... to want to

Unterhaltung   Entertainment

die Disco (s) .... disco
das Kino (s) .... cinema
das Konzert (e) .... concert
die Party (s) .... party
das Restaurant (s)......... restaurant
das Theater (-) .... theatre

Eintrittskarten kaufen   Buying tickets

die Band (s) .... pop group, band
die Eintrittskarte (n) .... ticket
der Eintrittspreis (e)..... entrance (cost)
die Ermäßigung (en).... reduction
der Erwachsene (n) ‡... adult
das Kind (er) .... child
das Parkett .... stalls (theatre)
der Platz (Plätze) .... seat
der Preis (e) .... cost, price

im ersten Rang............ in the circle (theatre)
der Schüler (-) .... school student
die Schülerermäßigung school student rate
die Schülerin (nen) ...... school student
der Student (en) *wk*...... university student
die Studentin (nen) ...... university student

Wann fängt es an? What time does it start?
am Abend.................... in the evening
an Feiertagen.............. on bank holidays
am Morgen.................. in the morning
am Nachmittag .... in the afternoon
die Öffnungszeiten *pl* .. opening times
um ein Uhr .... at one o'clock
die Stunde (n)............. hour

geöffnet...................... open
geschlossen .... closed

bis (+ acc) .... until
von (+ dat) .... from

Nützliche Verben   Useful verbs
anfangen *irreg sep* .... to start
ankommen* *irreg sep* .. to arrive
ausgehen* *irreg sep* ..... to go out
dauern .... to last
enden †....................... to end
kosten † .... to cost
lieben .... to love
spielen........................ to act
suchen .... to look for

For clock times see page 90
For numbers see page 88
For days of the week see page 89

FEIERTAGE

Wir feiern — We celebrate

Silvester................. New Year's Eve
das Neujahr.................. New Year's Day
Heilige Drei Könige... Twelfth Night
der Valentinstag........... St Valentine's Day
der Faschingsdienstag.. Shrove Tuesday
der Muttertag............... Mother's Day
Ostersonntag......... Easter Day
der erste Mai............... May 1st
Allerheiligen.......... All Saints (Nov 1st)
der Heiligabend........... Christmas Eve
der erste Weihnachtstag... Christmas Day

Chanukka............... Chanukah
Diwali.................... Divali
Id........................... Eid
das jüdische Neujahr.... Rosh Hashana
das Passa..................... Passover
Ramadan............... Ramadan
der Sabbat.................... Sabbath

die Bar-Mizwa............. Bar Mitzvah
die Flitterwochen *pl*..... honeymoon
die Geburt (en)........... birth
der Geburtstag (e)........ birthday
die Hochzeit (en)......... wedding
das Hochzeitsessen....... reception
der Namenstag (e)........ name day
die kirchliche Trauung. church wedding
die standesamtliche Trauung. civil ceremony

Allgemeines — General

der Ball (Bälle)........... ball
das Feuerwerk............. fireworks
die Geburtstagsparty (s)... birthday party
das Geschenk (e)......... present
die Geschichte (n)........ story, history
die Karte (n)............... card
der Kuchen (-)............ cake
die Musik.................. music

das Osterei (er).......... Easter egg
die Party (s)............... party
der Weihnachtsbaum (-bäume)
.... Christmas tree
der Weihnachtsmann (-männer)
.... Father Christmas
der Zug (Züge)........... procession

der Dom (e)................ cathedral
die Kirche (n)............. church
die Moschee (n).......... mosque
die Synagoge (n)......... synagogue

Leute — People

die Eltern *pl*............... parents
die Familie (n)............ family
der Freund (e)............. friend
die Freundin (nen)....... friend

der Christ (en) *wk*........ Christian
der Hindu (s)............... Hindu
der Jude (n) *wk*........... Jew
die Jüdin (nen)............ Jewess
der Muslim (s)............. Muslim
die Muslime (n).......... Muslim
der Sikh (s)................. Sikh

Wie war das? — What was it like?

Familien~.................... of the family
glücklich.................... happy
laut........................... noisy
religiös...................... religious

Nützliche Verben — Useful verbs

sich amüsieren †.......... to have a good time
Freunde besuchen †..... to visit friends
einladen *irreg sep*........ to invite
Freunde einladen *irreg sep*
.... to have friends round
essen *irreg*.................. to eat
feiern.......................... to celebrate
geben *irreg*................ to give

gehen* *irreg* .... to go
essen gehen* *irreg* .... to go to a restaurant
geschehen* *irreg* .... to happen
Musik hören .... to listen to music
kaufen .... to buy
schenken..................... to give a present
schicken...................... to send
singen *irreg* .... to sing
stattfinden *irreg sep* ..... to take place

tanzen......................... to dance
trinken *irreg* .... to drink
übernachten † .... to stay overnight

For other family words see page 27
For food see pages 53, 23
For recipes see page 55
For clothes see page 57

Redewendungen

Wo verbringst du Weihnachten/Chanukka/Diwali/Id? *Where do you spend Christmas/Chanukah/Divali/Eid?*

Was machst du? *What do you do?*

Was gibt es zu essen? *What do you have to eat?*

Bekommst du Geschenke? *Do you have presents?*

Ich schenke meinem Vater eine CD *I give my father a CD as a present*

Es hat Spaß gemacht *It was fun*

STADT UND LAND

Allgemeines General

das Dorf (Dörfer)......... village
die Industrie (n).......... industry
die Landwirtschaft....... agriculture
der Lärm..................... noise (unwelcome)
der Platz .... space
die Stadt (Städte)......... town
der Stadtrand .... edge of town
die Stille..................... silence, quiet
die Umgebung............ surroundings
die Umwelt................. environment
das Viertel (-).............. quarter
der Vorort (e).............. suburb, outskirts

Umgebung Geography

der Bach (Bäche)......... stream
der Berg (e) .... mountain
der Fluss (Flüsse) .... river
das Gebiet (e) .... region
das Gebirge (-) .... mountain range
der Hügel (-) .... hill
die Insel (n)................ island
das Klima (s) .... climate
das Land..................... country; countryside
die Provinz (en).......... province
die See (n).................. sea
der See (n).................. lake
das Tal (Täler)............. valley
die Talsperre (n).......... dam
die Wüste (n) .... desert

Leute   People

der Autofahrer (-) .... motorist
die Autofahrerin (nen) . motorist
der Bauer (n) *wk* .... farmer
die Bäuerin (nen) .... female farmer
der Briefträger (-) .... postman
die Briefträgerin (nen) . postwoman
die Einwohner *pl* .... inhabitants
der Fußgänger (-) .... pedestrian
der Händler (-) .... trader
die Händlerin (nen) ...... trader
die Kauffrau (en) .... businesswoman
der Kaufmann (-männer) . businessman
das Kind (er) .... child
der Ladenbesitzer (-) .... shopkeeper
die Ladenbesitzerin (nen) shopkeeper
der Landarbeiter (-) ..... farm worker
der Landwirt (en) .... farmer
der Polizist (en) *wk* ..... policeman
die Polizistin (nen) ...... policewoman
der Radfahrer (-) .... cyclist
die Radfahrerin (nen)... cyclist
der Stadtbewohner (-) .. city dweller

In der Stadt   In town
Gebäude   Buildings
der Bahnhof (-höfe) ..... station
die Bank (en) .... bank
das Büro (s) .... office
der Busbahnhof (-höfe) bus station
der Dom (e) .... cathedral
das Einkaufszentrum (-zentren)
.... shopping centre
die Fabrik (en) .... factory
der Flughafen (-häfen) . airport
das Geschäft (e) .... shop
das Hotel (s) .... hotel
das Informationsbüro (s) .. tourist office
die Jugendherberge (n) youth hostel
der Jugendklub (s) .... youth club
das Kino (s) .... cinema
die Kirche (n) .... church

das Krankenhaus (-häuser) ..... hospital
der Laden (Läden) .... shop
der Markt (Märkte) .... market
das Museum (Museen) .. museum
die Post .... post office
das Rathaus (-häuser) ... town hall
das Schwimmbad (-bäder) .. swimming pool
die Sparkasse (n) .... bank
das Theater (-) .... theatre

die Abtei (en) .... abbey
die Bibliothek (en) .... library
die Burg (en) .... castle (fortified)
die Eisbahn (en) .... ice rink
der botanische Garten (Gärten).. botanic
                          garden
die Klinik (en) .... clinic, hospital
das Polizeirevier (e) ..... police station
die Polizeiwache (n) ..... police station
das Postamt (-ämter) ..... post office
das Reisebüro (s) .... travel agency
das Schloss (Schlösser) . stately home
das Stadion (Stadien) .... stadium
die Tankstelle (n) .... petrol station
der Turm (Türme) .... tower
das Verkehrsamt (-ämter) . tourist office
der Wohnblock (s) .... block of flats

Orientierungspunkte Landmarks
die Altstadt .... town centre
die Ampel .... traffic lights,
                          pelican crossing
die Autobahn (en) .... motorway
die Brücke (n) .... bridge
die Bushaltestelle (n).... bus stop
der Campingplatz (-plätze) .... campsite
das Dorf (Dörfer) .... village
die Ecke (n) .... corner
die Fußgängerzone (n) . pedestrianised area
die Kreuzung (en) .... crossroads
der Ort (e) .... place
der Park (s) .... park
der Platz (Plätze) .... square

das Sportzentrum (-zentren).. sports centre
die Stadt (Städte) .... town
die Stadtmitte (n) .... town centre
die Straße (n) .... street
das Straßenende (n) ...... end of the road
die Telefonzelle (n) ..... phone box
das Viertel (-) .... district, area
der Vorort (e) .... suburb
der Zebrastreifen (-) ..... pedestrian crossing
der Zeitungskiosk (e) ... newspaper stand

die Allee (n) .... avenue (with trees)
der Bahnübergang (-gänge).. level crossing
der Briefkasten (-kästen) ...... letter box
der Bürgersteig (e) .... pavement
das Denkmal (-mäler) .. monument
der Hafen (Häfen) .... port
die Moschee (n) .... mosque
das Parkhaus (-häuser) . multi-storey car park
der Parkplatz (-plätze).. car park
die Sackgasse (n) .... cul de sac
der Stadtteil (e) .... part of a town
das Straßenschild (er)... road sign
die Synagoge (n) .... synagogue
der Tempel (-) .... temple
die U-Bahn .... underground
die Umgehungsstraße (n). ring road, bypass
die Unterführung (en).. subway
der Verkehr................ traffic
der Verkehrskreisel ..,,,. roundabout (traffic)

Im Park   In the park
die Bank (Bänke)........ bench
der Baum (Bäume)....... tree
die Blume (n) .... flower
das Blumenbeet (e) ...... flower bed
der Brunnen (-) .... fountain
der Kinderspielplatz (-plätze).....play area
die Schaukel (n).......... swing
die Wiese (n) .... grassed area

Auf dem Land   In the country
der Bauernhof (-höfe).. farm
der Baum (Bäume) ...... tree
die Blume (n) .... flower
das Dorf (Dörfer)........ village
das Feld (er) .... field (arable)
das Ferienhaus (-häuser) ...holiday cottage,
                                              second home
der Fluss (Flüsse) .... river
das Gras...................... grass
die Hecke (n) .... hedge
der Hügel (-) .... hill
das Land.................... countryside
die Natur.................... nature
der Obstgarten (-gärten) ...orchard
das Ufer (-) .... riverbank
der Traktor (en) .... tractor
der Wald (Wälder)....... forest, wood
der Wanderweg (e) ...... footpath
die Wiese (n) .... field (pasture)

Auf dem Bauernhof   On the farm
der Anhänger (-)......... trailer
der Bauer (n) *wk* .... farmer
die Bäuerin (nen) .... female farmer
das Bauernhaus (-häuser)..farmhouse
der Bauernhof (-höfe).. farm
die Ernte (n) .... harvest
das Heu .... hay
der Hof (Höfe) .... farmyard
   landwirtschaftliche Produkte *pl*
   .... farm produce
das Nest (er) .... nest
die Scheune (n) .... barn
der Stall (Ställe) .... stable
das Stroh .... straw
der Teich (e).............. pond
die Vogelscheuche (n). scarecrow
der Weinbauer (n) *wk* .. wine grower
der Weingarten (-gärten) ..vineyard
die Windmühle (n) ...... windmill

For animals see pages 30, 85

Wie ist es?	**What is it like?**
alt	old
angenehm	pleasant
benachbart	nearby, neighbouring
breit	wide
ehemalig	ex-, former
entzückend	charming
gefährlich	dangerous
groß	big
gut	good
hässlich	ugly
historisch	historic
industriell	industrial
interessant	interesting
klein	small
langweilig	boring
lebhaft	lively
malerisch	picturesque
mehrere	several
modern	modern
in der Nähe	near
natürlich	natural
ruhig	quiet
sauber	clean
schmutzig	dirty
schön	pretty, beautiful
still	peaceful
traurig	sad
verschmutzt	polluted
viel	a lot of, many
wichtig	important

Wo ist es?	**Where is it?**
in (+ dat)	in, at
um (+ acc)	around
neben (+ dat)	next to
gegenüber (+ dat)	opposite

hinter (+ dat)	behind
vor (+ dat)	in front of
zwischen (+ dat)	between
links von (+ dat)	on the left of
rechts von (+ dat)	on the right of
in der Nähe von (+ dat)	near
10 Kilometer von (+ dat)	entfernt
	10 km from ...
weit von (+ dat)	a long way from
in der Mitte von (+ dat)	in the middle of
an (+ dat)	on, near, beside
entlang (+ acc)	along
unter (+ dat)	under
ganz in der Nähe von (+ dat)	very near
hier in der Gegend	near here
dort drüben	over there
geradeaus	straight on

For countries see page 87

Nützliche Verben	**Useful verbs**
abbiegen* *irreg sep*	to turn
sich befinden *irreg*	to be situated
besuchen †	to visit
entschuldigen †	to excuse
bis ... gehen* *irreg*	to go as far as
nehmen *irreg*	to take
sehen *irreg*	to see
überqueren *insep* †	to cross
an (+ dat) vorbeigehen* *irreg sep*	
	to go past
weiterfahren* *irreg sep*	to drive on, continue
weitergehen* *irreg sep*	to walk on, continue

For weather see page 49

For shops see page 52

For holiday words see page 76

Redewendungen

Ich wohne seit zehn Jahren in Malvern *I have lived in Malvern for ten years*

Malvern ist eine Kleinstadt in der Nähe von Worcester *Malvern is a little town near Worcester*

Was gibt es in Malvern zu sehen? *What is there to see in Malvern?*

Es gibt die Berge, ein kleines Museum, einen Park und eine große Kirche *There are the hills, a small museum, a park and a big church*

Man kann ins Theater, ins Kino oder ins Hallenbad gehen *You can go to the theatre, the cinema or the swimming pool*

Man kann auf den Bergen spazieren gehen *You can go for walks on the hills*

DAS WETTER

Allgemeines   General

das Satellitenbild (er) ... satellite picture

die Vorhersage (n) .... forecast

die Wetterlage (n) .... weather conditions

die Wettervorhersage (n) ...... weather forecast

der Wetterbericht (e).... weather report

das Gewitter (-) .... thunderstorm

der Grad .... degree

der Himmel.................. sky

die Höchsttemperatur (en) ... highest temperature

der Nebel (-) .... fog

der Regen .... rain

der Schauer (-) .... shower, downpour

der Schnee .... snow

die Sonne (n) .... sun

der Sturm (Stürme) ...... storm

die Temperatur (en) ..... temperature

die Tiefsttemperatur (en) ... lowest temperature

der Wind (e) .... wind

die Wolke (n) .... cloud

die Aufheiterung (en) .. bright period

der Blitz (e) .... flash of lightning

der Donner.................. thunder

der Druck.................... pressure

der Dunst .... mist, haze

die Ebbe .... low tide

das Eis .... ice

die Feuchtigkeit........... dampness, humidity

die Flut....................... high tide

der Hagel.................... hail

die Hitze..................... heat

der Hochdruck............. high pressure

das Klima (s) .... climate

das Meer (e)................ sea

der Mond (e) .... moon

der Niederschlag......... precipitation
(rain or snow)

der Regenbogen (-bögen) rainbow

der Schatten................ shadow, shade

die See (n).................. sea

die Sichtweite............. visibility

der Sonnenaufgang (-gänge) sunrise

der Sonnenschein........ sunshine

der Sonnenuntergang (-gänge) . sunset

der Stern (e) .... star

der Tiefdruck.............. low pressure

die Verbesserung (en).. improvement

Die Jahreszeiten   Seasons

der Herbst................... autumn

der Frühling................ spring

der Sommer	summer	heute	today
der Winter	winter	manchmal	sometimes
		morgen	tomorrow
das Jahr (e)	year	neulich	recently
die Jahreszeit (en)	season	oft	often
der Monat (e)	month	übermorgen	the day after tomorrow
der Vormittag (e)	morning		
der Morgen (-)	morning	**Adjektive**	**Adjectives**
der Nachmittag (e)	afternoon	angenehm	pleasant
die Nacht (Nächte)	night	besser	better
der Abend (e)	evening	bewölkt	cloudy
		blau	blue

Wie ist das Wetter?
What is the weather like?

Es ist 30 Grad	It is 30 degrees
Es ist dunkel	It is dark
Es ist heiß	It is hot
Es ist hell	It is light
Es ist kalt	It is cold
Es ist neblig	It is foggy
Es ist niederschlagsfrei	It is dry
Es ist schön	It is fine
Es ist sonnig	It is sunny
Es ist stürmisch	It is stormy
Es ist windig	It is windy
Es ist wolkig	It is cloudy
Das Wetter ist schlecht	The weather is bad
Es blitzt	It is lightning
Es donnert	It is thundering
Es friert	It is freezing
Es hagelt	It is hailing
Es regnet	It is raining
Es schneit	It is snowing
Es gibt Frost	There is frost
Es gibt Gewitter	There are thunderstorms
Es gibt Nebel	There is fog
Es gibt Schnee	There is snow

diesig	misty, hazy
furchtbar	awful
heiß	hot
kalt	cold
klar	clear
mäßig	moderate
mild	mild
nächst	next
nass	wet
regnerisch	rainy
schlecht	bad
schön	fine
schwül	heavy, sultry
selten	rare
sonnig	sunny
stark	strong
stürmisch	stormy
trocken	dry
trüb	gloomy, dull
veränderlich	variable
wolkig	cloudy

Nützliche Verben   **Useful verbs**

bersten* *irreg*	to burst
donnern	to thunder
frieren *irreg*	to freeze
regnen †	to rain
scheinen *irreg*	to shine
schmelzen *irreg*	to melt
schneien	to snow
verändern †	to change

Wann?   **When?**

ab und zu	from time to time
gestern	yesterday
gewöhnlich	usually

vorhersagen *sep* .... to forecast	kälter werden* *irreg* .... to get colder
wehen .... to blow (wind)	mild werden* *irreg* ...... to become mild

WEGBESCHREIBUNGEN

Wie komme ich am besten ...?
How do I get to ...?

Entschuldigen Sie, bitte Excuse me
Wo ist ...? .... Where is ...?
Vielen Dank .... Thank you very much

Gehen Sie geradeaus! .. Go straight on
Gehen Sie die Straße entlang!
.... Go up/down the street
Nehmen Sie die B52! ... Take the B52

Nehmen Sie die erste Straße rechts!
.... Take the first on the right
Biegen Sie rechts ab! ... Turn right
Biegen Sie links ab! ..... Turn left
Gehen Sie über die Straße! Cross the road

Wo ist das?   **Where is it?**

an der Ampel vorbei .... after the crossroads
an der Straßenecke .... on the corner of the
                                            street
ganz in der Nähe .... close by
gegenüber der Bank ..... opposite the bank
hier in der Nähe .... near here
hinter dem Theater .... behind the theatre
in der Nähe vom Platz . near the square
neben der Post .... next to the post office
vor dem Kino .... outside the cinema
weit vom Bahnhof entfernt
.... a long way from the station
zwischen der Brücke und der Ampel
.... between the bridge and the lights

For Landmarks see page 46

Schilder   **Signs**

Anlieger frei .... residents only
bitte einordnen .... get in lane
den Rasen nicht betreten .. keep off the grass
Einbahnstraße .... one way street
Fußgängerzone .... pedestrians only
Halteverbot .... no stopping
keine Zufahrt .... no entry
Parkverbot .... no parking
Rad fahren verboten .... no cycling
rechts fahren .... keep to the right
Straße gesperrt .... road closed
Umleitung .... diversion

Die Landkarte   **The map**

die Autobahn (en) .... motorway
die Bundesstraße (n) .... A road, trunk road
die Landstraße (n) .... B road, country road
die Nebenstrecke (n) .... parallel route (HR)

Nützliche Verben **Useful verbs**

abbiegen* *irreg sep* ..... to turn off
fahren* *irreg* .... to go, travel
fahren *irreg* .... to drive (car)
gehen* *irreg* .... to go, walk
kennen *irreg* .... to know (place)
nehmen *irreg* .... to take (a route)
sehen *irreg* .... to see
überqueren *insep* .... to cross
weiterfahren* *irreg sep* to continue
wissen *irreg* .... to know (fact, how to)

For town words see page 46
For shops see page 52
For address words see page 10
For car and public transport see pages 63

Redewendungen

Wie kommt man am besten zum Bahnhof, bitte? *What is the best way to the station, please?*

Wo ist der Busbahnhof? *Where is the bus station?*

Ist es weit? *Is it far?*

Wie weit ist es? *How far is it?*

Es ist zehn Gehminuten weg *It's a ten minute walk*

Es ist fünf Kilometer entfernt *It's five kilometres*

Kann man mit dem Bus dahin fahren? *Can we get there by bus?*

Muss ich mit dem Taxi fahren? *Do I have to take a taxi?*

EINKAUFEN

Allgemeines   General

das Einkaufszentrum (-zentren)

.... shopping centre

das Geschäft (e) .... shop

der Laden (Läden) .... shop

die Stadtmitte (n) .... town centre

der Stadtrand (-ründe) .. outskirts

der Vorort (e) .... suburb

Leute   People

der Kassierer (-) .... cashier

die Kassiererin (nen) ... cashier

der Kunde (n) *wk* .... customer

die Kundin (nen) .... customer

der Geschäftsführer(-).. manager

die Geschäftsführerin (nen) .. manager

der Markthändler (-) .... market trader

die Markthändlerin (nen) . market trader

der Vorübergehende (n) ‡ passer-by

der Verkäufer (-).......... sales assistant

die Verkäuferin (nen) .. sales assistant

Die Geschäfte   The shops

die Bank (en)............. bank

das Kaufhaus (-häuser) department store

der Markt (Märkte)...... market

die Post .... Post Office

die Sparkasse (n) .... savings bank

der Supermarkt (-märkte) .supermarket

der Zeitungsstand (-stände)....news stand

die Apotheke (n) .... chemist's shop
(dispensing)

die Bäckerei (en)........ baker's shop

die Buchhandlung (en) bookshop

das Delikatessengeschäft (e) ..delicatessen

die Drogerie (n)........... chemist's shop
(non-dispensing)

die Eisenwarenhandlung (en)
.... ironmonger's shop

das Fischgeschäft (e) ... fish shop

das Fotogeschäft (e)..... photographer's

der Friseursalon (s)...... hairdresser's salon

die Gemüsehandlung (en) .greengrocer's

das Juweliergeschäft (e) ....jeweller's shop

das Kleidergeschäft (e) clothes shop

die Konditorei (en) ...... cake shop, sweet shop

das Lebensmittelgeschäft (e) .... grocer's shop
die Metzgerei (en) .... butcher's shop
die Molkerei (en) .... dairy
die Obsthandlung (en) . fruit seller's
der Optiker (-) .... optician
die Optikerin (nen) ...... optician
die Reinigung .... dry cleaner's
das Reisebüro (s) .... travel agency
das Schreibwarengeschäft (e) stationer's shop
die Selbstbedienung..... self service
der Tabakwarenladen (-läden)
.... tobacconist's shop
der Tante-Emma-Laden (Läden)
.... convenience store, corner shop
die Weinhandlung (en) wine merchant's

Im Geschäft   In the shop

die Abteilung (en) .... department
der Artikel (-) .... article
der Aufzug (-züge) ...... lift
die Ausstellung (en)..... display
die Kasse (n) .... cash desk
der Einkaufswagen (-).. trolley
das Erdgeschoss .... ground floor
das Etikett (en) .... label
der Fahrstuhl (-stühle).. lift
der Fensterladen (-läden) ...... shop window
das Geschoss (-e) .... floor
der Händler (-) .... shopkeeper
die Händlerin (nen) ...., shopkeeper
der Haupteingang (-gänge) main entrance
der Korb (Körbe) .... basket
die Lebensmittel *pl* ...... groceries
die Marke (n) .... make, brand
der oberste Stock .... top floor
der Preis (e) .... price
das Produkt (e) .... product
die Qualität (en) .... quality
die Quittung (en) .... receipt
das Regal (e) .... shelf
die Rolltreppe (n) .... escalator
der Stock (Stöcke) .... floor

der Umkleideraum (-räume) ..changing room
das Untergeschoss .... basement
die Waren *pl* .... goods

Schilder, Hinweise Signs, Notices

an der Kasse bezahlen . pay at the cash desk
aus zweiter Hand .... second-hand
Ausgang .... exit
bitte nicht berühren ..... please do not touch
drücken .... push
Eingang .... entrance
geschlossen .... closed
hier erhältlich .... on sale here
Notausgang .... emergency exit
Öffnungszeiten *pl* .... opening hours
Preisknüller .... fantastic prices
Preisnachlass .... reductions
Schlussverkauf .... sale
Selbstbedienung .... self-service
Sonderangebot............ on special offer
ziehen........................ pull
zu verkaufen............... for sale

Ich möchte ... . I would like ...
ab .... from (price)
Das geht .... That's fine
einige .... some (countable)
etwas .... some (uncountable)
genug .... enough
pro Person .... per person
viel............................. a lot of
Wie viel? .... How much?
Wie viele? .... How many?
Welche? .... Which?
zu viel .... too much
zu viele...................... too many

Lebensmittel kaufen   Buying food

Die Getränke   Drinks

der Alkohol .... alcohol
die Cola...................... cola
der Fruchtsaft (-säfte) .. fruit juice

der Kaffee.................... coffee
die Limonade .... lemonade
die Magermilch .... skimmed milk
die Schokolade .... chocolate
der Tee .... tea
die Vollmilch .... full milk
der Wein..................... wine

Bäckereiprodukte   **Bakery products**
der Berliner (-)............ doughnut
das Brot .... bread
das Brötchen (-) .... bread roll
der Keks (e) .... biscuit
der Kuchen (-) .... cake
die Torte (n) .... gateau

Lebensmittel   **Groceries**
das Bonbon (s) .... sweet
die Butter .... butter
die Chips *pl* .... crisps
das Ei (er) .... egg
das Eis .... ice cream
der Essig..................... vinegar
die Flakes *pl* .... cornflakes
die Gewürze *pl* .... spices
der Honig .... honey
der Joghurt (s) .... yoghurt
der Käse .... cheese
die Margarine .... margarine
die Marmelade (n) .... jam
das Mehl .... flour
die Nudeln *pl* .... pasta, noodles
das Öl .... oil
die Orangenmarmelade marmalade
die Pastete (n)............. pâté
der Pfeffer .... pepper (spice)
der Reis .... rice
die Sahne.................... cream
das Salz .... salt
der Senf...................... mustard
die Suppe (n) .... soup
der Zucker .... sugar

Fleisch   **Meat**
der Braten.................... joint, roast meat
die Ente (n) .... duck
die Frikadelle (n)........ rissole
das Geflügel .... poultry
das Hackfleisch........... mince
das Hähnchen .... chicken
das Hammelfleisch ...... mutton
das Hirschfleisch .... venison
das Kalbfleisch .... veal
das Kaninchen .... rabbit
das Kotelett (e) .... chop, cutlet
das Lammfleisch......... lamb
das Rindfleisch .... beef
die Salami .... salami
der Schinken............... ham
das Schweinefleisch..... pork
das Steak (s) .... steak
der Truthahn (-hähne).. turkey
die Wurst (Würste)...... sausage, salami, pâté

Gemüse   **Vegetables**
der Blumenkohl........... cauliflower
die Bohne (n) .... bean
die dicke Bohne (n) ..... broad bean
die grüne Bohne (n)..... green bean
die Erbsen *pl* .... peas
die Gurke (n)............... cucumber; gherkin
die Karotte (n) .... carrot
die Kartoffel (n) .... potato
der Kohl .... cabbage
der Kopfsalat.............. lettuce
der Pilz (e).................. mushroom
der Rosenkohl *no pl*..... Brussels sprout(s)
der Salat .... salad; lettuce
die Tomate (n)............. tomato
die Zwiebel (n)........... onion

die Aubergine (n) .... aubergine
die Avocado (s) .... avocado
die rote Beete (n)........ beetroot
der Brokkoli .... broccoli
der Knoblauch............. garlic

der rote/grüne Paprika.. red/green pepper
der Porree (s) .... leek
das Radieschen (-)........ radish
das Sauerkraut .... pickled cabbage
der Spargel .... asparagus
der Spinat .... spinach
die Zucchini *pl* .... courgettes
der Mais..................... sweetcorn

Obst   **Fruit**
die Ananas (-).............. pineapple
der Apfel (Äpfel) .... apple
die Apfelsine (n).......... orange
die Aprikose (n).......... apricot
die Banane (n) .... banana
die Birne (n) .... pear
die Brombeere (n)........ blackberry
die Erdbeere (n).......... strawberry
die Grapefruit (s) .... grapefruit
die Haselnuss (-nüsse) . hazelnut
die Himbeere (n) .... raspberry
die rote Johannisbeere (n) redcurrant
die schwarze Johannisbeere (n)
.... blackcurrant
die Kirsche (n)............ cherry
die Kiwi (s) .... kiwi
die Limone (n)............ lime
die Mandarine (n) .... tangerine
die Melone (n) .... melon
die Nektarine (n) .... nectarine
der Pfirsich (e) .... peach
die Pflaume (n)........... plum; prune
die Stachelbeere (n) ..... gooseberry
die Walnuss (-nüsse).... walnut
die Weintraube (n)....... grape
die Zitrone (n) .... lemon

Fisch   **Fish**
die Fischstäbchen *pl* .... fish fingers
die Forelle (n).............. trout
der Hering (s) .... herring
der Hummer (-)............ lobster
der Kabeljau .... cod

die Krabbe (n) .... shrimp
der Krebs (e) .... crab
der Lachs.................... salmon
die Muscheln *pl*.......... mussels
der Räucherlachs .... smoked salmon
die Sardine (n)............ sardine
der Schellfisch............ haddock
die Scholle (n)............. plaice
der Thunfisch (e) .... tuna

Wie ist es?   **What is it like?**
ausgezeichnet .... excellent
Bio˗ .... organic
bitter.......................... bitter
frisch.......................... fresh, not frozen
gebraten .... roast, fried
gedunstet .... steamed
gefüllt......................... stuffed
gegrillt........................ grilled, barbecued
gekocht...................... boiled; cooked
getoastet .... toasted
gut .... good; well
gut durchgebraten........ well-cooked (roast/fried)
halb˗ .... half
hausgemacht............... home-made
heiß........................... hot
kalt............................ cold
lecker .... delicious
lokal .... local
Öko˗ .... environmentally
                 friendly
roh .... raw
salzig......................... salty; savoury
sauber........................ clean
sauer.......................... sour
schlecht .... bad
süß .... sweet

Rezepte   Recipes
Wie macht man das?
         How do you make that?
das Basilikum .... basil
die Gewürze *pl* .... spices

der Ingwer .... ginger
der Knoblauch .... garlic
die Petersilie .... parsley
der Pfeffer .... pepper (spice)
der Rosmarin .... rosemary
die Salbei .... sage
der Salz .... salt
der Schnittlauch .... chives
der Thymian .... thyme
der Zimt..................... cinnamon

auf kleiner Flamme...... on a low heat
bei mäßiger Hitze .... in a moderate oven
gebuttert .... buttered
gehackt .... minced
gekocht...................... boiled
gerieben...................... grated
gewürzt .... spicy
gut .... thoroughly
paniert .... breaded
roh .... raw, uncooked

Nützliche Verben   Useful verbs
abschmecken *sep* .... to flavour
man braucht................ you need, take
bräunen .... to brown, fry gently
füllen......................... to fill
gießen *irreg* .... to pour
kochen....................... to cook
kochen lassen *irreg* ...... to bring to the boil
mischen...................... to mix
rollen......................... to roll
schälen .... to peel
schlagen *irreg* .... to beat
schneiden *irreg* .... to cut
vorbereiten † *sep* .... to prepare
würzen....................... to season
zerschneiden *irreg* .... to cut up
zudecken *sep* .... to cover

einen Kaffeelöffel........ a teaspoonful
einen Esslöffel............. a tablespoonful
eine Prise................... a pinch of

Maße und Gewichte   Weights and measures
ein Dutzend................ dozen
100 Gramm .... 100 grams of
das Gramm................. gram
das Kilo...................... kilo
der Liter .... litre
einen halben Liter........ half a litre of
das Pfund................... pound (lb)
ein halbes Pfund......... half a pound

die Hälfte (n).............. half
das Drittel.................. third
das Viertel .... quarter

die Dose (n) .... tin, can
die Flasche (n)............ bottle
das Glas...................... jar, pot
ein paar .... a few
ein Paar (e)................. a pair
die Packung (en) .... packet
die Scheibe (n) .... slice
das Stück .... piece; item
die Tube..................... tube

Bezahlen   Paying
der Euro .... euro
die Mark..................... DM
der Groschen (-) .... 10Pf piece, Austrain coin
der Schilling............... Austrian Schilling
der Franken (-) .... Swiss franc
der Pfennig................. Pf, German coin
das Pfund................... £, pound sterling
die Währung (en) .... currency

die Brieftasche (n) .... wallet
die Euroscheckkarte (n)....Eurocheque card
der Fünfzigmarkschein (e) 50 Mark note
das Geld .... money
die Kasse (n) .... cash desk, till
das Kleingeld.............. change
die Kreditkarte (n)....... credit card
die Münze (n).............. coin
das Portemonnaie (s) ... purse

der Preis (e) .... price
das Scheckheft (e) .... cheque book
der Strichcode (s) .... barcode
das Taschengeld .... pocket money

Kleidung kaufen   Buying clothes

die Mode (n) .... fashion
die Größe (n) .... size

der BH (s) .... bra
die Bluse (n) .... blouse
das Hemd (en) .... shirt
die Hose (n) .... pair of trousers
die Jacke (n) .... jacket
die Jeans .... pair of jeans
das Kleid (er) .... dress
die Krawatte (n) .... tie
die Leggings *pl* .... leggings
der Mantel (Mäntel) ..... coat, overcoat
die Shorts *pl* .... pair of shorts
der Pullover (-) .... pullover
der Pulli (s) *coll* .... pullover
der Rock (Röcke) .... skirt
der Schuh (e) .... shoe
der Slip (s) .... pair of knickers
die Socke (n) .... sock
die Strumpfhose (n) ..... pair of tights
das Sweatshirt (s) .... sweatshirt
das T-Shirt (s) .... T-shirt
der Trainingsanzug (-züge) ... tracksuit
die Turnschuhe *pl* .... trainers
die Unterhose (n) .... pair of underpants

der Anorak (s) .... anorak
der Anzug (Anzüge) .... (gents) suit
der Badeanzug (-anzüge) . swimsuit
die Badehose (n) .... swimming trunks
der Bikini (s) .... bikini
der Bademantel (-mäntel) dressing gown
der Gürtel (-) .... belt
der Handschuh (e) .... glove
der Hausschuh (e) .... slipper

der Hut (Hüte) .... hat
das Kostüm (e) .... (ladies) suit
die Latzhose (n) .... dungarees
das Nachthemd (en) ..... nightdress
der Regenmantel (-mäntel) ...raincoat
die Sandale (n) .... sandal
der Schal (s) .... scarf
der Schlafanzug (-anzüge) .....pair of pyjamas
der Schlips (e) .... tie
der Stiefel (-) .... boot
die Weste (n) .... waistcoat

die Armbanduhr (en) ... watch
der Ärmel (-) .... sleeve
die Gürteltasche (n) ..... bumbag
das Haarband (-bänder) scrunchie
die Halskette (n) .... necklace
der Knopf (Knöpfe) ..... button
der Kragen (-) .... collar
die Ohrringe *pl* .... earrings
der Regenschirm (e) .... umbrella
der Reißverschluss (-schlüsse) ...zip
der Ring (e) .... ring
die Tasche (n) .... pocket; bag
das Taschentuch (-tücher) handkerchief
das Tuch (Tücher) .... headscarf

Material   Material

aus Baumwolle .... made of cotton
aus Gold .... made of gold
aus Kunstfaser .... made of man-made
                           fibres
aus Leder .... made of leather
aus Metall .... made of metal
aus Seide .... made of silk
aus Silber .... made of silver
aus Wolle .... made of wool

Make-up   Make-up

das Mascara .... mascara
der Lidschatten .... eye shadow
das Parfüm .... perfume
der Lippenstift (e) .... lipstick
der Nagellack .... nail varnish

Wie ist es? What is it like?

ähnlich...................... similar
aus zweiter Hand .... second hand
billig........................... cheap
dunkel .... dark (colour)
eng .... tight; narrow
etwas Billigeres .... something cheaper
etwas Schönes .... something pretty
frisch .... cool, fresh
ganz.......................... whole, complete
gestreift .... striped
günstig...................... good value (of prices)
hell .... light (colour)
kostenlos .... free
kurz........................... short
lang .... long
leicht .... light (weight); easy
neu .... new
preiswert.................... good value
teuer.......................... expensive, dear
verschieden................ different

For colours see page 29

For numbers see page 88

Welche Größe? What size is it?
Für Frauen For women

das Kleid (er) .... dress
das Kostüm (e)............. suit
der Pullover (-) .... jumper
Größe 36 .... size 10
Größe 38 .... size 12
Größe 40 .... size 14
Größe 42 .... size 16
Größe 44 .... size 18
klein .... small
mittelgroß................... medium
groß........................... large

Für Männer For men

der Anzug (-züge)........ suit
die Jacke (n) .... jacket
Größe 46 .... size 36
Größe 48 .... size 38

Größe 50 .... size39-40
Größe 52 .... size 42
Größe 54 .... size 44

das Hemd (en) .... shirt
Größe 36 .... size 14
Größe 37 .... size 14½
Größe 38 .... size 15
Größe 39/40 .... size 15½
Größe 41 .... size 16

Welche Schuhgröße haben Sie? What size shoes do you take?

Größe 37 .... size 4
Größe 37.5 .... size 4½
Größe 38 .... size 5
Größe 39 .... size 5½
Größe 39.5 .... size 6
Größe 40 .... size 6½
Größe 40.5 .... size 7
Größe 42 .... size 8
Größe 43 .... size 9
Größe 44.5 .... size 10
Größe 45.5 .... size 11
Größe 47 .... size 12

All European sizes given are approximate

Für wen ist das? Who is it for?

Das ist für mich.......... It's for me
Das ist ein Geschenk ... It's for a present

Beschwerden Complaints

die Batterie (n) .... battery
die Beschwerde (n)...... complaint
das Leck (s) .... leak
das Loch (Löcher) .... hole
die Quittung (en) .... receipt
die Überschwemmung (en)....flood
die Waschanleitung ..... washing instructions

Adjektive Adjectives

eingelaufen................. shrunk
enttäuscht .... disappointed
fertig .... ready

gebrochen .... broken
geklemmt .... jammed, stuck
gerissen .... torn
kaputt .... broken, not working
möglich .... possible
nett .... kind
praktisch .... practical
rein .... clean
sauber .... clean
schlecht .... bad
schmutzig .... dirty
stark .... strong, solid
unmöglich .... impossible
verstopft .... blocked
zu breit .... too wide
zu eng .... too tight, too narrow
zu groß .... too big
zu kurz .... too short
zu teuer .... too expensive

Was funktioniert nicht?
What is broken/not working?

die Armbanduhr (en) ... watch
der CD-Spieler (-) .... CD player
der Computer (-) .... computer
der Fotoapparat (e) ...... camera
die Spülmaschine (n) ... dishwasher
die Taschenlampe (n) .. torch
die Waschmaschine (n) washing machine

Wen soll ich anrufen?
Who shall I ring?

der Besitzer (-) .... owner
die Besitzerin (nen) ..... owner
der Elektriker (-) .... electrician
der Geschäftsführer (-) . manager
die Geschäftsführerin (nen)   manager
der Klempner (-) .... plumber
der Mechaniker (-) .... mechanic
die Werkstatt (-stätten) garage

Nützliche Verben   Useful verbs

sich beschweren † .... to complain
brechen *irreg* .... to break
bringen *irreg* .... to bring
einwickeln *sep* .... to wrap up, gift wrap
fallen lassen *irreg* .... to drop
funktionieren † .... to work, function
hassen........................ to hate
kaufen .... to buy
kontrollieren † .... to check
kosten † .... to cost
nehmen *irreg* .... to take
prüfen........................ to check
rechnen † .... to add
Das reicht .... That's enough
reparieren † .... to mend, repair, fix
versprechen *irreg*........ to promise
vorbereiten † *sep* .... to prepare
wollen *irreg* .... to wish, want
zurückkommen* *irreg sep* to come back
zurücknehmen *irreg sep* .. to take back

akzeptieren † .... to accept
auswählen *sep* .... to choose
behalten *irreg* .... to keep
beweisen *irreg* .... to prove
bieten *irreg* .... to offer, give (present)
einlaufen* *irreg* .... to shrink
gewährleisten † .... to guarantee
kritisieren † .... to criticise
leihen *irreg* .... to borrow
messen *irreg* .... to measure
reinigen lassen *irreg* .... to have cleaned
reißen *irreg* .... to tear, rip
reparieren lassen *irreg* . to have mended
schulden † .... to owe
teilen .... to divide
trauen .... to trust, entrust
vorschlagen *irreg sep* .. to suggest
vorziehen *irreg sep* ...... to prefer
wiegen *irreg* .... to weigh
zählen........................ to count
zusammenrechnen † *sep* .. to add up

Redewendungen

Sie sagen:

Entschuldigung, ist hier in der Nähe eine Apotheke? *Excuse me, is there a chemist nearby?*

Haben Sie ...? *Do you sell ...?*

Ich möchte lieber... *I would prefer...*

Ich nehme das *I'll take this*

Was kostet das? *How much is it?*

Muss ich an der Kasse bezahlen? *Do I have to pay at the cash desk?*

Ich habe kein Kleingeld *I have no change*

Ich habe nur einen Fünfzigmarkschein *I've only got a 50 mark note*

Darf ich diesen Pullover anprobieren? *May I try on this jumper, please?*

Es ist zu groß/zu eng/zu klein *It's too big/too tight/too small*

Darf ich mit Kreditkarte bezahlen? *May I pay by credit card?*

Können Sie es einwickeln, bitte? *Can you gift-wrap it for me, please?*

Das ist alles, danke *That's all, thank you*

Der Verkäufer/die Verkäuferin sagt:

Wer ist dran? *Who is next?*

Kann ich Ihnen helfen? *May I help you?*

Sonst noch etwas? *Anything else?*

Haben Sie Kleingeld? *Have you any change?*

Welche Größe haben Sie? *What size are you?*

Probleme:

Es gibt einen Fehler *There is a mistake*

Ich möchte diesen Pullover wechseln *I would like to change this pullover*

Ich habe die Quittung behalten *I have kept the receipt*

Die Farbe steht mir nicht *The colour does not suit me*

Entschuldigung, die Socken haben nicht dieselbe Größe *Excuse me, these socks are different sizes*

Ich bin der Anleitung gefolgt, aber dieser Pullover ist eingelaufen *I followed the washing instructions, but this jumper has shrunk*

Diese Armbanduhr funkioniert nicht *This watch doesn't work*

DIENSTLEISTUNGEN

Auf der Post	**At the post office**
die Adresse (n)	address
der Brief (e)	letter
der Briefkasten (-kästen)	letter box
die Briefmarke (n)	stamp
der Briefträger (-)	postman
die Briefträgerin (nen)	postwoman
das Formular (e)	form
die letzte Leerung	the last collection
die nächste Leerung	the next collection
das Päckchen (-)	small parcel
das Paket (e)	parcel
das Porto	postage
die Post	post office; mail
das Postamt (-ämter)	post office
die Postanweisung (en)	postal order
die Postkarte (n)	postcard
die postlagernde Sendung	poste restante
der Schalter (-)	counter position
der Tabakhändler (-)	tobacconist
der Tag (e)	day
die Telefonkarte (n)	phone card
die Woche (n)	week

Wie viel?	How much?
Wie viele?	How many?
Wie lange?	How long?
dringend	urgent
verloren	lost
per Einschreiben	by registered post
per Luftpost	by air mail
ins Ausland	(to) abroad

In der Bank	**At the bank**
der Ausweis (e)	ID
die Bank (en)	bank
der Euro	euro
der Euroscheck (s)	Eurocheque
der Franken (-)	Swiss franc
der Fünfzigmarkschein (e)	50 mark note

das Geld	money
der Geldautomat (en) *wk*	cash machine
der Groschen (-)	10Pf piece; Austrian coin
die Kasse	till
das Kleingeld	change
das Konto (s)	account number
die Kreditkarte (n)	credit card
die Mark	DM
der Pass (Pässe)	passport
das Pfund	£ sterling
die Provision (en)	commission
Prozent	per cent
der Reisescheck (s)	travellers' cheque
das Scheckheft (e)	cheque book
die Scheckkarte (n)	cheque card
der Schilling	Austrian Schilling
die Währung (en)	currency
der Wechselkurs (e)	exchange rate
die Wechselstube (n)	bureau de change
das Zweimarkstück (e)	a two mark coin

Nützliche Verben	**Useful verbs**
akzeptieren †	to accept
anrufen *irreg sep*	to phone
ein Formular ausfüllen *sep*	to fill in a form
benutzen †	to use
einen Scheck einlösen *sep*	to cash a cheque
einwerfen *irreg sep*	to post
an die Kasse gehen* *irreg*	to go to the cash desk
sich irren	to make a mistake
die Post zustellen *sep*	to deliver the post
Provision nehmen *irreg*	to charge commission
schicken	to send, post
unterschreiben *irreg insep*	to sign
wechseln	to change
weiterschicken *sep*	to send on
zahlen	to count

Fundsachen　　Lost property

die Brieftasche (n) .... wallet
das Fahrrad (-räder) ..... bicycle, bike
der Fotoapparat (e) ...... camera
die Handtasche (n) .... handbag
die Kamera (s) .... video camera
der Koffer (-) .... case
das Portemonnaie (s) .... purse
der Regenschirm (e) ..... umbrella
der Rucksack (-säcke) .. rucksack
das Scheckheft (e) .... cheque book
der Schlüssel (-) .... key

eine Art .... a sort of
der Ausweis (e) .... ID
die Belohnung (en) ...... reward
die Beschreibung (en) .. description
das Datum (Daten) .... date
die Farbe (n) .... colour
das Formular (e) .... form
die Gebühr (en) .... fee
die Gestalt (en) .... shape
die Größe .... size
die Marke (n) .... make
der Paß (Pässe) .... passport
der Schaden .... damage

For materials see page 57

Nützliche Verben　　Useful verbs

ausfüllen *sep* .... to fill in
berichten † .... to report
bieten *irreg* .... to offer
fahren* *irreg* .... to travel
fallen lassen *irreg* .... to drop
finden *irreg* .... to find
gehen* *irreg* .... to go
liegen lassen *irreg sep* . to leave behind
legen .... to put (down flat)
stecken .... to put (in something)
stehlen *irreg* .... to steal
stellen........................ to put (upright)
suchen........................ to look for
vergessen *irreg* .... to forget
verlieren *irreg* .... to lose
zeigen........................ to show

For telephone words see page 74
For money words see page 75
For other office words see page 71

Redewendungen

Ich möchte dieses Paket nach Großbritannien schicken *I would like to send this parcel to Britain*
Was kostet ein Brief nach Großbritannien, bitte? *How much does it cost to send a letter to Britain?*
Fünf Briefmarken zu einer Mark, bitte *Five stamps at 1 Mark, please*
Ich habe meinen Fotoapparat/meine Tasche/mein Portemonnaie verloren *I've lost my camera/my bag/my purse*
Ich habe ihn/sie/es im Zug liegen lassen *I left it in the train*
Man hat mir die Brieftasche gestohlen *I've had my wallet stolen*
Muss ich zur Polizeiwache gehen? *Do I have to go to the police station?*
Ich bin hier fremd *I am not from this area*
Ich bin auf Urlaub *I am on holiday*

VERKEHRSMITTEL

Allgemeines	General
die Abfahrt (en)	departure
die Ankunft (-künfte)...	arrival
das Ausland	abroad
die Fahrt (en)..............	journey
der Feiertag (e)	public holiday
die Ferien *pl*	holidays
die Reise (n)	journey
das Willkommen..........	welcome, reception

Verkehrsmittel	Means of transport
das Auto (s)	car
der Bus (se)	bus
der Dampfer (-)............	steamer, riverboat
das Fahrrad (-räder)	bicycle, bike
das Flugzeug (e)...........	plane
der Hubschrauber (-)....	helicopter
die alte Kiste (n)	banger (car)
der Lastwagen (-).........	lorry
der Lieferwagen (-)......	van
das Luftkissenboot (e)..	hovercraft
das Mofa (s)	moped
das Motorrad (-räder)...	motorbike
das Mountainbike (s)....	mountain bike
der Reisebus (se).........	coach
die Straßenbahn (en)....	tram
die U-Bahn (en)	underground, metro
die öffentlichen Verkehrsmittel *pl*	public transport
der Wagen (-)	car
der Zug (Züge)	train

Leute	People
der Autofahrer (-)	motorist, driver
der Bahnbeamte (n) ‡...	railway official
der Fahrer (-)	driver
die Fahrerin (nen)	driver
der Fußgänger (-).........	pedestrian
der LKW-Fahrer (-)	lorry driver
der Mechaniker (-)	mechanic

der Passagier (e)	passenger
der Pilot (en) *wk*	pilot
der Polizist (en) *wk*.....	policeman
die Polizistin (nen)	policewoman
der Radfahrer (-).........	cyclist
die Radfahrerin (nen) ..	cyclist
der Reisende (n) ‡	traveller
der Schaffner (-)	ticket collector
der Steward (s)	steward
die Stewardess (-en)	air stewardess
der Tankwart (e)	pump attendant
der Tourist (en) *wk*	tourist
die Touristin (nen).......	tourist

Bahnreisen	Train travel
die Abfahrt (en)..........	departure
das Abteil (e)	compartment
die Ankunft	arrival
die Auskunft...............	information
die Bahn.....................	railway
der Bahnhof (-höfe)	railway station
der Bahnsteig (e)	platform
der Eilzug (-züge)........	regional express train
die einfache Fahrkarte (n) single ticket
die Fahrkarte (n).........	ticket
der Fahrkartenschalter (-) ticket office
der Fahrplan (-pläne) ...	timetable
das Gepäck	luggage
das Gepäckschließfach (-fächer)	left luggage locker
das Gleis (e)................	platform, track no
der ICE-Zug (-Züge) ...	Inter-City train
der Inter-Regio	regional express
erster Klasse	first class
zweiter Klasse	second class
der Liegewagen (-)	couchette car
der Nichtraucher.........	non-smoker
der Personenzug (-züge) ..	slow train
die Reservierung (en) ..	reservation
die Rückfahrkarte (n) ..	return ticket

der Schlafwagen (-) ..... sleeping car

der Schnellzug (-züge) . express train

der Speisewagen (-) ..... dining car, buffet (car)

der Taxistand .... taxi rank

die Verbindung (en) .... connection

die Verspätung (en) ..... delay

der Wagen (-) .... carriage

der Wartesaal (-säle) .... waiting room

das Ziel (e) .... destination

der Zug (Züge) .... train

Bus und Straßenbahn
Bus and tram travel

der Busbahnhof (-höfe) bus station

die Bushaltestelle (n) ... bus stop

der Entwerter (-) .... ticket validating machine

die Fahrkarte (n) .... ticket

der Fahrkartenautomat (en) *wk*
.... ticket vending machine

der Fahrpreis (e) .... fare

der Lautsprecher (-) ..... loudspeaker

die Linie (n) .... line, route

die Nummer (n) .... number

die Streifenkarte (n)..... book of tickets

die Zehnerkarte (n) ...... book of ten tickets

Die Überfahrt   Crossing the Channel

die Fähre (n) .... car ferry

der Fährhafen (-häfen) . ferry terminal

der Hafen (Häfen) .... port

der Kanaltunnel .... Channel Tunnel

das Meer (e) .... sea

das Schiff (e) .... boat

die Überfahrt (en) .... crossing

glatt .... smooth

pünktlich .... on time

seekrank .... seasick

stürmisch .... rough (crossing)

verspätet .... late

Flugreisen   Flying

die Ansage (n) .... call

der Flug (Flüge) .... flight

der Flughafen (-häfen) . airport

der Flugsteig (e) .... gate

das Flugzeug (e) .... plane

der Jumbojet (s) .... jumbo jet

die Kabine (n) .... cabin

die Landung (en) .... landing

die Pünktlichkeit .... punctuality

der Sicherheitsgurt (e) . seat belt

die Touristenklasse...... tourist class

die Verspätung (en)..... delay

Autofahren   Going by car

die Ampel .... traffic lights

die Autobahn (en) .... motorway

das Autobahnnetz .... motorway network

die Hauptstraße (en) .... main road

die Landstraße (n) .... secondary road

die Nebenstrecke (n) ... alternative route

die Ausfahrt .... motorway exit

die Baustelle (n) .... roadworks

das Ende (n) .... end

die Gefahr (en) .... danger

die Geschwindigkeit (en).......speed

die Hauptverkehrszeit (en) ....rush hour

die Kreuzung (en) .... crossroads

die Kurve (n) .... bend

die Landkarte (n) .... map

der LKW (s) .... HGV, lorry

das Öl .... oil

das Parkhaus (-häuser) . multi-storey car park

der Parkplatz (-plätze) . car park

der PKW (s) .... car

der Rastplatz (-plätze).. picnic area

der Stau (s) .... traffic jam, delay

die Tankstelle (n) .... garage, petrol station

die Tiefgarage (n)........ underground car park

die Toilette (n) .... toilets

die Umleitung (en) ...... diversion
die Werkstatt (-stätten) garage (repairs)

der Bürgersteig (e) .... pavement
die Fahrschule (n) .... driving school
der Führerschein (e) ..... driving licence
die Gebühr (en) .... toll
der Helm (e) .... helmet
das Kennzeichen (-) ..... number plate
der Mittelstreifen (-) .... central reservation
die Parkscheibe (n) ...... parking disc
der Schülerlotse (n) *wk* ... school crossing patrol
die Straßenmarkierung (en) .. road markings
das Straßenschild (er)... road sign
die Straßenverkehrsordnung . highway code
der Verkehrskreisel ...... roundabout
die Versicherung .... insurance
die Versicherungspolice (n) .. insurance policy
die Vorfahrt................ right of way, priority
der zähflüssige Verkehr ... slow-moving traffic

Ich habe eine Panne
     My car has broken down
der Auspuff.................. exhaust pipe
der Autoschlüssel (-).... car key
die Batterie (n) .... battery
die Bremse (n) .... brake
das Geräusch (e) .... noise (quiet-ish)
der Lärm..................... noise (loud)
die Marke (n).............. make
der Motor (en) .... engine
die Panne (n) .... breakdown
der Pannendienst.......... breakdown service
der Platten .... puncture
der Reifen (-) .... tyre
der Scheinwerfer (-)..... headlight
der Tank (s) .... petrol tank
das Warnlicht (er) .... warning light
die Windschutzscheibe (n).... windscreen

der Blinker (-).............. indicator
das Ersatzrad (-räder)... spare wheel
das Ersatzteil (e) .... spare part

der Gang (Gänge) .... gear
das Gas(pedal) .... accelerator
das Getriebe (n) .... gearbox
die Haube (n) .... bonnet
die Hupe (n) .... horn
der Katalysator (en) ..... catalytic converter
der Kofferraum (-räume) . boot
der Kühler (-) .... radiator
die Kupplung (en) .... clutch
das Lenkrad (-räder) .... steering wheel
der Rückspiegel (-) ...... rear view mirror
die Scheibe (n) .... window
die Scheibenwischer *pl* ... windscreen wipers
das Schloss (Schlösser) ... lock
die Schlussleuchten *pl* . rear lights
der Sicherheitsgurt (e) . seat belt
die Stoßstange (n)........ bumper

Nützliche Verben   **Useful verbs**
anrufen *irreg sep* .... to phone
funktionieren † .... to work
halten *irreg*................. to stop
kaputt gehen* *irreg* ..... to break down
platzen*..................... to burst (tyre)
reparieren † .... to fix, repair
warten † auf (+ acc)..... to wait for

An der Tankstelle
     At the petrol station
das Benzin .... petrol
   bleifreies Benzin.... unleaded petrol
   verbleites Benzin ... leaded petrol
der Diesel .... diesel
die Dose Öl .... can of oil
das Frostschutzmittel ... anti-freeze
das Getränk (e) .... drink
die Landkarte (n)........ map
der Liter .... litre
die Luft .... air
das Öl .... oil
der Reifendruck.......... tyre pressure
der Stand .... level

65

Super bleifrei......... super unleaded
der Tankwart.............. pump attendant
die Tankwärtin (nen) ... pump attendant
das Wasser................ water

Ein Unfall   **An accident**

Leute   **People**
der Arzt (Ärzte)........... doctor
der Autofahrer (-)........ car driver
die Autofahrerin (nen). cyclist
der Feuerwehrmann (-männer). fireman
der Fußgänger (-)......... pedestrian
die   Krankenschwester (n)........ nurse
der Krankenwagenfahrer (-)
.... ambulance driver
der Motorradfahrer (-) . motorcyclist
der Passant (en) *wk*...... passer-by
der Polizist (en) *wk*...... policeman
Herr Wachtmeister. "officer"
der Zeuge (n) *wk*......... witness
die Zeugin (nen)......... witness

Allgemeines   **General**
die Adresse (n)............ address
die Ausrede (n)............ excuse
die Aussage (n)............ statement
der Autounfall (-fälle).. car accident
die Erlaubnis (se)........ permission
die erste Hilfe............ first aid
das Fahrzeug (e) .... vehicle
die Gefahr (en) .... danger
der Knall.................... impact
der Krankenwagen (-).. ambulance
die Polizei *sing* .... the police
die Polizeiwache (n) .... police station
das Problem (e)........... problem
das Pusteröhrchen........ breath test device
der Reisebus (-se) .... coach
die Richtung (en)......... direction
das Risiko (Risiken)..... risk
der Schaden................ damage
die Schuld .... fault
die Straßenverkehrsordnung . highway code

die Tragbahre (n) .... stretcher
die Vorfahrt................. priority
der Zusammenstoß (-stösse) ..collision, pile-up

Ist es ernst?   **Is it serious?**
ängstlich..................... anxious
bewusstlos.................. unconscious
dringend..................... urgent
ernst........................... serious
erstaunlich.................. surprising
falsch .... wrong
langsam...................... slowly
schnell........................ quick
im Schock .... in shock
tot .... dead
verletzt....................... injured

Ausrufe   **Exclamations**
Abgemacht!................. OK, agreed!
Ach!............................ Oh!
Das macht nichts!........ Never mind!
Feuer!......................... Fire!
Hilfe! .... Help!
Meine Güte! .... My goodness!
Pass auf!..................... Look out!
Umso besser!.............. So much the better!
Verzeihung! .... Sorry!

Nützliche Verben   **Useful verbs**
benutzen †.................. to use
dauern .... to last
entwerten †................. to time stamp a ticket
fahren* *irreg* .... to go (vehicle)
fliegen* *irreg* .... to fly (person)
gehen* *irreg* .... to walk, go on foot
auf Deck gehen* *irreg* . to go up on deck
holen.......................... to fetch
kaufen .... to buy
landen* †.................... to land
laufen* *irreg* .... to walk
mieten † .... to hire
mit dem Auto fahren* *irreg* ...to go by car
mit dem Bus fahren* *irreg*.....to go by bus

mit dem Rad fahren* *irreg*.... to go by bike
mit dem Reisebus fahren* *irreg*
.... to go by coach
nach Hause fahren* *irreg*...... to return home
starten* †...................... to take off (plane)
suchen .... to look for

abfahren* *irreg sep*...... to leave (from)
ankommen* *irreg sep* .. to arrive
aussteigen* *irreg sep* ... to get off/out of
einsteigen* *irreg sep*.... to get on/into
mit dem Zug fahren* *irreg*.... to go by train
sich informieren † über (+ acc)
.... to find out about
kontrollieren † .... to examine, check
den Zug nehmen *irreg* . to catch the train
umsteigen* *irreg sep*.... to change trains
verpassen † .... to miss (train, etc)
warten † auf (+ acc)..... to wait for

anhalten* *irreg sep* ...... to stop

den Motor anlassen *irreg sep*
.... to start the engine
die Scheinwerfer anmachen *sep*
.... to switch on the headlights
den Motor ausmachen *sep*
.... to switch off the engine
die Reifen aufpumpen *sep*
.... to pump up the tyres
bremsen...................... to brake
fahren *irreg* .... to drive (a vehicle)
rückwärts fahren* *irreg* ... to reverse
eine Panne haben *irreg* ... to break down
hupen .... to sound the horn
nachsehen *irreg sep* ..... to check
parken .... to park
den Gang schalten † .... to change gear
überholen *insep* .... to overtake
überqueren *insep* .... to cross
voll tanken *sep* .... to fill up with petrol
langsamer werden* *irreg* . to slow down
zusammenstoßen* mit (+ dat) *irreg sep*
.... to collide with, bump into

Redewendungen

Der Zug fährt von Gleis 8 ab *The train leaves from platform 8*
Der Zug fährt um halb eins ab *The train leaves at 12.30 midday*
Muss ich umsteigen? *Do I have to change?*
Einmal hin und zurück, zweiter Klasse, bitte *I would like a second class return, please*
Wo kann ich parken? *Where can I park?*
Dreißig Liter bleifrei, bitte *30 litres of lead-free, please*
Ich habe eine Panne *My car has broken down*
Der Motor springt nicht an *The engine will not start*
Ich fliege von Birmingham nach München *I am flying from Birmingham to Munich*

AUSBILDUNG UND BERUF

Prüfungen und danach
Exams and afterwards

Allgemeines   **General**

die Antwort (en) .... answer

die falsche Antwort ..... wrong answer

die richtige Antwort .... right answer

die Arbeit .... work

das Examen (-) .... degree exam

die Frage (n) .... question

die Konzentration .... concentration

die Note (n) .... mark

die Prüfung (en) .... exam

die mündliche Prüfung speaking test

die schriftliche Prüfung writing test

Leute   **People**

der Auszubildende (n) ‡... trainee

der Bewerber (-) .... applicant

die Bewerberin (nen) ... applicant

der Lehrer (-) .... teacher

die Lehrerin (nen)........ teacher

der Lehrling (e) .... apprentice

der Prüfer (-) .... examiner

der Schüler (-) .... school student

die Schülerin (nen) ...... school student

der Student (en) *wk* ..... university student

die Studentin (nen) ...... university student

Adjektive   **Adjectives**

gruppenmäßig.............. as a group

individuell .... individual

langweilig................... boring

letzt .... last

lustig .... amusing, "fun"

nächst .... next

schwer........................ difficult

Nützliche Verben   **Useful verbs**

arbeiten †.................... to work

die Frage beantworten †
.... to answer the question

eine Prüfung bestehen *irreg* ...to pass an exam

durchfallen* *sep* .... to fail an exam

lernen.......................... to learn, study (at school)

eine Prüfung nehmen *irreg* ....to take an exam

pauken *coll*.................. to revise, swot

studieren †................... to study (at university)

vorbereiten † *sep* .... to prepare for

In der Oberstufe   **In the Sixth Form**

das Abitur................... A level/GNVQ Level 3

die Berufsschule (n) .... technical college

der Hauptschulabschluss (-schlüsse)
.... GNVQ Level 1

die Klausur (en) .... end of module test

der Kurs (e) .... course

die humanistischen Fächer *pl*
..............................literary studies; humanities

die Naturwissenschaften *pl* ....sciences

die Neusprache (n) ...... modern language

das Niveau (s).............. level

das Oberstufenkolleg (-ien)
.... VIth form or tertiary college

der Realschulabschluss (-schlüsse)
.... GCSE/GNVQ Level 2

der Unterricht ...... teaching

Höhere Bildung   Higher education

die Hochschule (n) ...... university

die Musikakademie ..... academy of music

die Pädagogische Hochschule...College of HE

das Staatsexamen (-) .... degree

die Universität (en)...... university

Ausbildung   Training

die Ausbildung........... training scheme

die Berufsausbildung... vocational training

das Berufsvorbereitungsjahr
.... youth training scheme

die Lehre (n) .... apprenticeship

die Volkshochschule (n) ...evening classes

der Wettbewerb (e) ...... competition

Nützliche Verben   Useful verbs

sich ausbilden lassen *irreg*
.... to go on a training course
ausgebildet werden* *irreg*
.... to receive training

ein gutes Zeugnis haben *irreg*
.... to have good references
Staatsexamen machen.. to graduate
studieren †................... to read for a degree

ARBEITSSUCHE

Allgemeines   General

die Arbeitslosigkeit...... unemployment
die Aushilfsarbeit (en) . temporary work
der Beruf (e) .... career, profession
der Betrieb (e)............. business, firm
die Firma (Firmen) ...... firm
der Führerschein (e)..... driving licence
das Gehalt (Gehälter) ... salary
das Geschäft (e) .... business
der Handel .... trade
der Job (s)................... (unskilled, student) job
der Lohn (Löhne)......... pay, wages
die Persönlichkeit (en). personality, character
die Stelle (n)............... job, post
die Summe (n)............ sum of money
das Team (s) .... team
die Teilzeitarbeit (en) .. part-time work
die Vollzeitarbeit (en).. full-time work

Die Bewerbung   Applying for a job

die Ausbildung .... professional training
der Brief (e) .... letter
der Familienname (n) *wk* . surname
der Familienstand .... family status
das Geburtsdatum .... date of birth
der Geburtsort (e) .... place of birth
die Handschrift .... handwriting
der Lebenslauf .... CV, curriculum vitae
die Schreibweise.......... spelling
das Staatsexamen (-) .... degree
der Vorname (n) *wk* ..... first name

Nützliche Verben   Useful verbs

arbeiten † .... to work
ausgeben *irreg sep*....... to give, hand out
beraten *irreg*.............. to advise
bestätigen † .... to confirm
einen Kurs machen...... to go on a course

Leute   People at work

NB The feminine version of a profession is not
given where it is formed by adding -**in (nen)** to
the masculine noun.

der Angestellte (n) ‡.... employee
der Arbeitgeber (-)....... employer
der Arbeitnehmer (-).... employee
der Arbeitslose (n) ‡.... unemployed person
der Auszubildende (n) ‡ .. apprentice
der Chef (s) .... boss
der Direktor (en)......... director, manager
der Geschäftsführer (-) manager
der Gewerkschaftler (-) trade unionist
der Kollege (n) *wk* .... colleague
die Kollegin (nen) .... colleague
der Lehrling (e) .... apprentice
die Leitung.................. management
der Personalleiter (-) .... personnel director
der Sekretär (e)........... secretary
der Streikende (n) ‡..... striker
der Verkaufsleiter (-) ... sales and marketing
director

Berufe   Jobs

NB The feminine version of a profession is not given where it is formed by adding **-in (nen)** to the masculine noun.

Gängige Berufe   Common professions

der Arzt (Ärzte) .... doctor

die Ärztin (nen) .... doctor

der Beamte (n) ‡ .... civil servant, official

der Designer (-) .... designer

der Informatiker (-) ...... computer scientist

der Ingenieur (e) .... engineer

der Journalist (en) *wk* ... journalist

der Krankenpfleger (-) . male nurse

die Krankenschwester (n) nurse

der Lehrer (-) .... teacher

der Musiker (-) .... musician

der Politiker (-) .... politician

der Programmierer (-) .. programmer

der Rechtsanwalt (-anwälte) .. lawyer

die Rechtsanwältin (nen) . lawyer

der Schulleiter (-) .... headteacher

der Sozialarbeiter (-) .... social worker

der Steuerberater (-) ..... accountant

der Tierarzt (-ärzte) ..... vet (fem like Arzt)

der Zahnarzt (-ärzte) .... dentist (fem like Arzt)

Seltenere Berufe   Less common professions

der Architekt (en) *wk* ... architect

der Autor (en) *wk* .... writer

der Berater (-) .... consultant (not doctor)

der Bibliothekar (e) ...... librarian

der Chirurg (en) *wk* ...... surgeon

der Dolmetscher (-) ...... interpreter

der Forscher (-) .... research worker

der Maler (-) .... painter

der Meteorologe (n) *wk* meteorologist

der Moderator (en) .... TV presenter

der Naturwissenschaftler (-) .. scientist

der Physiotherapeut (en) *wk* .. physiotherapist

Gewerbetreibende   High street professions

der Apotheker (-) .... chemist (dispensing)

der Bäcker (-) .... baker

der Drogist (en) *wk* ...... chemist (non-dispensing)

der Fischhändler (-) ..... fishmonger

der Fleischer (-) .... butcher

der Florist (en) *wk* .... florist

der Fotograf (en) *wk* .... photographer

die Friseuse (n) .... hairdresser

der Frisör (e) .... hairdresser

der Gemüsehändler (-) . greengrocer

der Hotelbesitzer (-) .... hotelier

der Kassierer (-) .... till operator, cashier

der Ladenbesitzer (-) ... shopkeeper

der Obsthändler (-) ...... fruitseller

der Verkäufer (-) .... sales assistant

der Wohnungsmakler (-)...estate agent

der Zeitungshändler (-) newsagent

Handwerker   Skilled workers

der Bauunternehmer (-) builder

der Bergmann (Bergleute) ..miner

der Büroangestellte ‡... office worker

der Chef (s) .... boss

der Elektriker (-) .... electrician

der Fahrer (-) .... driver

der Fischer (-) .... fisherman

der Gärtner (-) .... gardener

die Geschäftsfrau (en) . businesswoman

der Geschäftsmann (-männer) ...businessman

der Handwerker (-) ...... craftsman, tradesman

der Kellner (-) .... waiter

der Klempner (-) .... plumber

der Koch (Köche) .... cook

die Köchin (nen) .... cook

der Maurer (-) .... bricklayer

der Mechaniker (-) .... mechanic

die Sekretärin (nen) ..... secretary

der Techniker (-) .... technician

der Tischler (-) .... carpenter

Andere Arbeiten   Other occupations

der Arbeiter (-) .... manual worker

der Ausbilder (-) .... instructor

der Bauer (n) *wk* .... farmer

der Briefträger (-) .... postman
der Feuerwehrmann (Feuerwehrleute)
.... fireman
die Hausfrau (en) .... housewife
der Hausmann (-männer) . house-husband
der Hausmeister (-) ...... caretaker
der Matrose (n) *wk* .... sailor
der Pilot (en) *wk* .... pilot
der Polizist (en) *wk* ..... policeman
der Rettungsschwimmer (-)... lifeguard
der Sänger (-) .... singer
der Schiedsrichter (-) ... referee
der Soldat (en) *wk* .... soldier
die Stewardess (-en) .... air hostess

Der Arbeitsplatz   The workplace

das Büro (s) .... office
die Fabrik (en) .... factory
die Firma (Firmen) ...... firm
das Geschäft (e) .... shop
das Krankenhaus (-häuser) .... hospital
das Labor (s) .... laboratory
der Laden (Läden) .... shop
die Schule (n) .... school

drinnen .... outdoors
draußen..................... indoors

Im Büro   In the office

der Anrufbeantworter (-).. answering machine
die Besprechung (en)... meeting
das Blatt Papier........... sheet of paper
die Briefmarke (n) .... stamp
der Briefumschlag (-schläge) envelope
der Computer (-) .... PC, computer
das Fax (-) .... fax
das Faxgerät (e) .... fax machine
die Faxnummer (n) ...... fax number
das Formular (e) .... form
die Gewerkschaft (en).. union
die Heftklammer (n) .... staple
die Heftmaschine (n) ... stapler

der Locher................. hole punch
die Post .... post, mail
der Tageslichtprojektor (en)
.... overhead projector
das Telefonbuch (-bücher) .....phone book
die Telefonnummer (n) phone number
der Termin (e) .... appointment
der Terminkalender (-) diary
die Tinte (n) .... ink

Schilder und Hinweise
Signs and Notices

Anmeldung................. reception
Aufzug...................... lift
Ausgang..................... way out, exit
Damen....................... ladies' toilets
Drücken .... push
Eingang..................... entrance
Empfang.................... reception
Gefahr...................... danger
Geschlossen................ closed
Herren....................... gents' toilets
Kein Eintritt .... no entry
Notausgang .... emergency exit
00 .... toilets
Offen......................... open
Rauchen verboten........ no smoking
Sekretariat................. secretary's office
Vorsicht Stufe .... mind the step
Ziehen....................... pull

Vorteile und Nachteile
Advantages and disadvantages

die Arbeitszeit............ hours of work
die sedentäre Arbeit..... a sitting down job
eine Arbeit im Freien... outdoor work
die Büroarbeit .... indoor work

Nützliche Verben   Useful verbs

abends arbeiten †........ to work evenings
draußen arbeiten † .... to work outdoors
drinnen arbeiten †........ to work indoors

71

ganztags arbeiten † ...... to work full-time

halbtags arbeiten † .... to work part-time

mit Computer arbeiten † .. to use a computer

mit Ziffern arbeiten † .. to work with figures

Tag und Nacht arbeiten †

.... to work day and night

am Wochenende arbeiten †

.... to work weekends

Landschaftspflege betreiben *irreg*

.... to work for conservation

Daten eingeben *irreg sep* . to key in data

forschen...................... to do research

zu Unfällen gehen* *irreg* . to go to the scene of
accidents

Kontakt mit Leuten haben *irreg*

.... to have a lot of contact with people

Leuten helfen *irreg* ...... to help people

reisen*...................... to travel

ins Ausland reisen*...... to travel abroad

Erfahrungen sammeln.. to broaden one's
experience

isoliert sein* *irreg* .... to be isolated

selbständig sein* *irreg* . to work for oneself

Uniform tragen *irreg* ... to wear a uniform

Text verarbeiten † .... to use a word
processor

Trinkgeld verdienen †.. to earn tips

reich werden* *irreg* ..... to get rich

Eigenschaften   Qualities

die Geduld.................. patience

die Geschicklichkeit .... dexterity

die Gesundheit............ good health

die Höflichkeit .... politeness

die Intelligenz .... intelligence

der Sinn für Humor ..... sense of humour

die Unermüdlichkeit.... inexhaustability

das Urteilsvermögen.... judgement

ehrlich........................ honest

erfahren...................... experienced

fleißig........................ hard-working

geduldig..................... patient

höflich........................ polite

intelligent................... intelligent

Nützliche Verben   Useful verbs

pünktlich ankommen* *irreg sep*

.... to arrive on time

arbeiten † .... to work

faxen......................... to fax, send a fax

Verspätung haben *irreg* to be late

sich für Informatik interessieren †

.... to be interested in IT

kündigen .... to sack, make redundant

den Kunden respektieren † ....to have respect
for the customer

arbeitslos sein* *irreg* ... to be unemployed

gut gekleidet sein* *irreg* ...to be well-dressed

gut organisiert sein* *irreg*

.... to be well-organised

streiken .... to go on strike

in den Ruhestand treten* *irreg*

.... to retire

verdienen † .... to earn

zusammenarbeiten † *sep* ...to co-operate

Redewendungen

Was wirst du nächstes Jahr machen? *What are you going to do next year?*

Ich werde die Schule verlassen *I'm going to leave school*

Ich werde bei meinem Vater auf dem Bauernhof arbeiten *I'm going to work on the farm with my
father*

Ich werde eine Lehre machen *I am going to do an apprenticeship*

Ich werde Neusprachen lernen *I'm going to do modern languages*

Ich möchte studieren *I would like to go to university*

DIE WERBUNG

Wo gibt es Werbung?
Where do you find advertising?

das Fernsehen .... television
die Illustrierte (n) ‡..... magazine
der Katalog (e)............. catalogue
die Litfaßsäule (n) .... advertising pillar
das Magazin (e) .... magazine
das Radio.................... radio
die Reklamewand (-wände)   hoarding
die Zeitschrift (en)....... magazine
die Zeitung (en).......... newspaper

Allgemeines   General

das Angebot (e)........... offer
die Belohnung (en) ...... reward
die Ferienwohnung (en)... holiday home
die Frische.................. freshness
die Geburt (en) .... birth
das Haus (Häuser) .... house
die Hochzeit (en) .... marriage (ceremony)
die Kleinanzeige (n) .... small ad
das Mountainbike (s).... mountain bike
die Nachfrage .... demand
      niedrige Preise *pl* ... low prices
das Produkt (e)............ products
das Rad (Räder) .... bike
das Sonderangebot (e).. special offer
der Tod (e).................. death
der Urlaub .... holidays
das Vergnügen .... pleasure
der Verkauf (-käufe) .... sale
der Wagen (-) .... car
der Werbespruch (-sprüche)
      .... advertising slogan
der Wert (e) .... value
die Wohnung (en)........ flat
die Zeitverschwendung waste of time

Adjektive   Adjectives

billiger....................... less expensive
dumm......................... stupid
funkelnagelneu .... brand new
interessant .... interesting
lehrreich..................... instructive
lustig .... amusing
neu .... new
nützlich .... useful
preiswert .... cheap, good value

im Angebot .... on offer
aus zweiter Hand .... second-hand
im Schlussverkauf .... in the sales
zu verkaufen............... for sale
zu vermieten............... for hire

Meiner Meinung nach
In my opinion

Es macht mich wütend It makes me angry
Ich finde es lustig .... I find it funny
Ich finde es langweilig I find it boring
Es geht mir auf die Nerven
      .... It gets on my nerves
Es bringt mich zum Lachen
      .... It makes me laugh

Nützliche Verben   Useful verbs

anbieten *irreg sep* .... to offer
ausnutzen *sep* .... to take advantage of
austauschen *sep* .... to exchange
forschen .... to research
kaufen .... to buy
einen Wunsch hervorrufen *irreg sep*
      .... to create a desire
mieten † .... to rent, hire
verkaufen † .... to sell
verlieren *irreg* .... to lose
wollen *irreg*................ to want

73

TELEFONIEREN

Allgemeines   General

der Anruf (e)............... phone call

der Anrufbeantworter (-).. answering machine

der Anrufer (-)............. caller

die Auskunft............... directory enquiries

die Telefonzelle (n) ..... call box

der e-mail-Anschluss ... e-mail address

die Faxnummer (n) ...... fax number

das Faxgerät (e) .... fax machine

der Handy (s).............. mobile phone

der Hörer (-) .... handset

die Münze (n).............. coin

das Münztelefon (e) ..... payphone

der Notruf (e) .... emergency call

die Nummer (n).......... number

das R-Gespräch (e) ...... transfer charge call

der Tarif (e) .... rate, charge

das Telefonbuch (-bücher) directory

die Telefonkarte (n)..... phonecard

das Tonzeichen .... dialling tone

die Vorwahl (en) .... code

die Zahl (en)............... figure, number

die Zentrale .... exchange, operator

am Apparat................. "speaking"; on the
                                    phone

Warten Sie auf das Tonzeichen!
.... Wait for the dialling code

Wählen Sie 110!.......... Dial 110 (Police,
                                    Ambulance, Fire)

falsch verbunden .... wrong number

defekt......................... out of order

Bitte, warten Sie! .... Hold the line

besetzt........................ engaged, busy

Wo bekommt man eine Telefonkarte?
Where can I get a phonecard?

auf der Post .... at the post office

beim Zeitungshändler.. at the newsagent's

an der Tankstelle .... at the petrol station

Nützliche Verben   Useful verbs

den Hörer abnehmen *irreg sep*
.... to lift the handset

anrufen *irreg sep* .... to phone (someone)

den Hörer auflegen *sep* ....to hang up

fragen......................... to ask

ein R-Gespräch führen. ....to make a transfer
                                    charge call

kaufen .... to buy

klingeln...................... to ring (of phone)

am Telefon sein* *irreg* ....to be on the phone

sprechen *irreg* .... to speak

telefonieren † .... to phone (in general)

wählen........................ to dial

zuhören *sep* .... to listen

zurückrufen *irreg sep* .. to call back

Redewendungen

Wo sind die Telefonbücher? *Where are the phone books?*

Sie sind neben den Kabinen *They are next to the phone booths*

Ist es ein Kartentelefon? *Is it a cardphone?*

Kann ich David sprechen, bitte? *Hello, may I speak to David, please?*

David am Apparat *David speaking*

Ich bin unterbrochen worden *I have been cut off*

Kann ich etwas ausrichten? *Would you like to leave a message?*

Sie werden am Telefon verlangt *You are wanted on the phone*

Um nach Großbritannien zu telefonieren, wählen Sie 00 44, dann die britische Vorwahl ohne die
Null, dann die Rufnummer *To phone the UK, dial 0044, then the area code without the 0, and
then the number*

DAS GELD

Allgemeines   General

das Bargeld .... cash
das Geld .... money
das Kleingeld .... small change
die Münze (n) .... coin

der Geldschein (e) .... note
das Taschengeld .... pocket money
die Währung (en) .... currency

die Bank (en) .... bank
die Börse (n) .... Stock Exchange
das Budget (s) .... budget
das Darlehen .... loan
der Geldautomat (en) *wk* .. cash dispenser
die Hypothek (en) .... mortgage
die Inflation (en) .... inflation
die Lebenshaltungskosten *pl*. cost of living
die Sparkasse (n) .... savings bank
der Geldwechsel .... currency exchange

der Euroscheck (s) .... Eurocheque
die Geheimzahl (en) .... PIN number
das Girokonto (-konten) ... current account
die Kreditkarte (n) .... credit card
der Reisescheck (s) ...... travellers' cheque

der Scheck (s) .... cheque
das Scheckheft (e) .... cheque book
die Scheckkarte (n) ...... banker's card
das Sparbuch (-bücher) savings account
der Wechselkurs .... exchange rate

der Dollar .... dollar
der Euro .... euro
die Mark .... German mark
das Pfund .... £, pound sterling
das irische Pfund .... Punt, Irish pound
der Schilling .... Austrian schilling
der Schweizer Franken Swiss franc

Nützliche Verben   Useful verbs

Geld ausgeben *irreg sep* .. to spend money
bezahlen † .... to pay (for)
kaufen .... to buy
leihen *irreg* .... to borrow, lend
wert sein* *irreg* .... to be worth
sparen .... to save up
in den roten Zahlen stehen *irreg*
.... to be in the red
wechseln .... to change (money)
zurückzahlen *sep* .... to pay back

FERIEN UND AUSFLÜGE

Allgemeines   General

das Datum (Daten) .... date
der Frühling .... spring
der Herbst .... autumn
der Monat (e) .... month
die Nacht (Nächte) ...... night
der Sommer .... summer
der Tag (e) .... day
der Winter .... winter
die Woche (n) .... week
For weather see page 49

Tourismus   Tourism

der Aufenthalt (e) .... stay
der Ausflug (-flüge) ..... outing
der Austausch (e) .... exchange
die Fahrt (en) .... journey
die Ferien *pl* .... holidays
die Gegend (en) .... region
Halbpension .... half board
die Kirmes .... funfair
die Klassenfahrt (en) ... school trip
der Nationalpark (s) ..... national park
das Picknick (s) .... picnic
der Preis (e) .... price
die Reise (n) .... journey
der Safaripark (s) .... safari park
der Spaziergang (-gänge) . walk
die Stille .... silence
die Überfahrt (en) .... crossing
die Unterkunft .... lodging
der Vergnügungspark (s) . amusement park
Vollpension .... full board
die Wanderung (en) ..... long walk

der Ausweis (e) .... identity card
der Bahnhof (-höfe) ..... station
die Bank (en) .... bank
die Broschüre (n) .... brochure
der Busbahnhof (-höfe) coach station

der Campingplatz (-plätze) ....camp site
die Ferienwohnung (en) ...holiday home
der Flughafen (-häfen). airport
das Foto (s) .... photo
der Fotoapparat (e) ...... camera
der Hafen (Häfen) .... port
das Hotel (s) .... hotel
das Informationsbüro (s) ...information office
die Jugendherberge (e) ....youth hostel
der Koffer (-) .... case
die Landkarte (n) .... map
die Mitgliedskarte (n) .. membership card
der Pass (Pässe) .... passport
die Pension (en) .... boarding house
der Reisescheck (s) ...... traveller's cheque
der Reiseveranstalter (-)....travel agent, tour
                                operator
der Rucksack (-säcke).. rucksack
der Stadtplan (-pläne) .. town plan
das Verkehrsamt (-ämter) .tourist office
der Videorekorder (-) .. camcorder
die Wechselstube (n) ... bureau de change
der Wohnwagen (-) ...... caravan
das Zelt (e) .... tent

Leute   People

der Besitzer (-) .... owner
die Besitzerin (nen) ..... owner
der Busfahrer (-) .... coach driver
die Busfahrerin (nen)... coach driver
der Camper (-) .... camper
die Empfangsdame (n) receptionist
die Herbergseltern *pl* ... youth hostel wardens
                                (couple)
die Herbergsmutter ..... youth hostel warden
der Herbergsvater .... youth hostel warden
der Kellner (-) .... waiter
die Kellnerin (nen) ...... waitress
der Leiter (-) .... group leader
die Leiterin (nen) .... group leader

der Rettungsschwimmer (-)... lifeguard
die Rettungsschwimmerin (nen) . lifeguard
der Tourist (en) *wk*....... tourist
die Touristin (nen)....... tourist
der Urlauber (-)........... holiday maker
die Urlauberin (nen) .... holiday maker

Einen Austausch mitmachen
Going on an exchange

der Ausflug (-flüge)..... outing
der Brieffreund (e)....... penfriend
die Brieffreundin (nen) penfriend
die Dauer.................... duration (stay, lesson)
das Essen .... food
die deutsche Familie.... German family
die englische Familie... English family
die Freizeit .... free time
die Hausaufgaben *pl* .... homework
die deutsche Küche...... German cooking
die englische Küche..... English cooking
der Lehrer (-).............. teacher
die Lehrerin (nen)........ teacher
das Lernprogramm (e) . curriculum
die Reise (n) .... journey
die Schule (n) .... school
die Schuluniform......... school uniform
der Sport.................... sport
die Stunde (n) .... lessons
das Taschengeld.......... pocket money

vergleichen *irreg* mit (+ dat)
.... to compare with

Jugendherberge   Youth hostel

der Abfalleimer (-)....... rubbish bin
die Bettwäsche............. linen
das Büro (s) .... office
die Decke (n) .... blanket
die Küche (n).............. kitchen
der Leinenschlafsack (-säcke)
.... sheet sleeping bag
der Schlafraum (-räume).. dormitory

der Schlafsack (-säcke) ... sleeping bag
der Speiseraum (-räume) . dining room
der Spielraum (-räume) ... games room
der Tagesraum (-räume) .. day room
heißes Wasser........ hot water
kaltes Wasser......... cold water

Campingplatz   Campsite

der Campingkocher (-) camping stove
der Campingplatz (-plätze)campsite
der Dosenöffner (-)..... tin opener
der Empfang................ reception
die Gasflasche (n)........ gas cylinder
die Lebensmittel *pl*...... food(stuff)s
die Luftmatraze (n)...... air bed
die Sanitäranlage (n) .. toilet block
der Schlafsack (-säcke) sleeping bag
der Stellplatz (-plätze) . pitch
die Streichhölzer *pl* ..... matches
der Strom .... electricity
die Taschenlampe (n) .. torch
das Taschenmesser (-).. pocket knife
(Kein) Trinkwasser...... (non) drinking water
die Waschmaschine (n) washing machine
der Wohnwagen (-)...... caravan
das Zelt (e) .... tent

der elektrische Anschluss. electric hook-up
das Camping................ camping
das Camping Carnet (s) ... camping carnet
die Campingausrüstung ... camping equipment
warmes Essen zum Mitnehmen
.... cooked take-away meals
das Fahrzeug (e) .... vehicle
das Lagerbett (en)........ camp bed
das Lagerfeuer (-) .... camp fire
der Radverleih............ cycle hire
das Spülbecken (-) .... washing up sink
die Steckdose (n)........ power point
die Wäsche................. washing (clothes)
die Wäscherei............. laundry
der Zuschlag (-schläge) supplement

Im Hotel At the hotel

die Anmeldung............ reception
das Bad........................ bath
das Bett (en) .... bed
das Doppelzimmer (-) .. double room
die Dusche (n) .... shower
das Einzelzimmer (-).... single room
das Erdgeschoss........... ground floor
der Fahrstuhl (-stühle) . lift
das Familienzimmer (-) family room
der Keller (-)................ basement
der Parkplatz (-plätze) . car park
der Preis (e) .... price
das Restaurant (s)......... restaurant
der Schlüssel (-)........... key
die Seife .... soap
der Stock (Stockwerke) storey
die Toiletten *pl* .... toilets
die Treppe (n).............. stairs
das Zimmer (-)............. room

das Doppelbett (en)...... double bed
der Eingang (-gänge) ... entrance
der Empfang (-fänge) .. reception
der Fernseher (-).......... TV set
das Formular (e) .... form
das Handtuch (-tücher). towel
der Kleiderbügel (-) ..... coathanger
der Kleiderschrank (-schränke) wardrobe
das Kopfkissen (-)........ pillow
das Laken (-)................ sheet
der Notausgang (-gänge).. (emergency) exit
das Telefon (e) .... telephone
die Übernachtung (en) . overnight stay
die Wolldecke (n)........ blanket

Wie lange? For how long?
der Tag (e) .... day
der Monat (e) .... month
die Nacht (Nächte) ...... night
die Woche (n)............. week

für drei Tage .... for three days
für vier Nächte .... for four nights
für zwei Wochen......... for a fortnight

Wieviele Personen? For how many?
der Erwachsene (n) ‡... adult
der Junge (n) *wk* .... boy
das Kind (er)............... child
das Mädchen (-)........... girl
die Person (en) .... person
bis drei Jahre.............. under three years old

Wann bist du gefahren? When did you go?
gestern........................ yesterday
vorgestern .... the day before yesterday
am Wochenende.......... at the weekend
letzte Woche .... last week
vor zwei Monaten........ two months ago
vor zwei Wochen .... a fortnight ago
letztes Jahr .... last year

Wann wirst du fahren? When will you be going?
zu Weihnachten........... at Christmas
zu Ostern.................... at Easter
im August .... in August
morgen........................ tomorrow
übermorgen................. the day after tomorrow
nächste Woche .... next week
in einer Woche........... in a week's time
in drei Monaten.......... in three months' time
in den Sommerferien... in the summer holidays
nächstes Jahr .... next year

Mit wem? With whom?
die Familie (n)............. family
der Freund (e)............. friend
die Freundin (nen)....... friend
der Brieffreund (e)....... penfriend
die Brieffreundin (nen) penfriend

Was hast du gegessen What did you eat?
der Bohnensalat.......... bean salad
das Brathähnchen........ roast chicken

die Brötchen *pl* .... breadrolls
die Currywurst .... sausage with curry
                     sauce
der Eintopf .... stew, casserole
der Hamburger .... hamburger
das Jägerschnitzel .... breaded pork steak
                     with mushrooms
die Käsetorte .... cheesecake
ein Lachsbrot .... a smoked salmon open
                     sandwich
die Leberwurst .... liver pâté
der Reibekuchen (-) ..... potato pancake
mit Sahne .... with cream
die Sauerkirschen *pl* .... sour cherries
das Sauerkraut .... sauerkraut
die bayrische Spezialität .. Bavarian speciality
   Würstchen mit Pommes
                     sausages and chips
die Zwiebelsuppe .... onion soup

For other foods see page 23, 53
For recipe words see page 55

Am Meer   At the seaside

die Angelrute (n) .... fishing rod
der Eimer (-) .... bucket
das Eis .... ice cream
der Eisverkäufer (-) ...... ice cream seller
der Kies .... shingle
der Liegestuhl (-stühle) deck chair
das Motorboot (e) .... motor boat
die Möwe (n) .... seagull
die Muschel (n) .... shells
der Rettungsring (e) ..... lifebelt
das Ruderboot (e) .... rowing boat
der Sand .... sand
die Sandburg (en) .... sandcastle
das Schlauchboot (e) .... inflatable dinghy
die See (n) .... sea
das Segelboot (e) .... dinghy
die Sonnenbrille (n) ..... sunglasses
der Sonnenhut (-hüte) .. sunhat
das Sonnenöl .... sun oil

der Strand (Strände) .... beach
der (un)überwachte Strand
                     (un)supervised beach
der Strandkorb (-körbe) wicker wind-break
das Surfbrett (er) .... sailboard
die Welle (n) .... wave (sea)

die Ebbe .... low tide
die erste Hilfe .... first aid
der Felsen (-) .... cliff
der Fischer (-) .... fisherman
das Fischerboot (e) ...... fishing boat
die Flut .... high tide
der Hafen (Häfen) .... port
die Jacht (en) .... yacht
der Jachthafen (-häfen) yacht marina
der Kai (s) .... quay
der Leuchtturm (-türme) .. lighthouse
das Segelschiff (e) .... sailing ship

Wintersport   Winter sports
Leute   **People**
der Anfänger (-) .... beginner
die Anfängerin (nen) ... beginner
der Führer (-) .... guide
die Führerin (nen) .... guide
der Skiläufer (-) .... skier
die Skiläuferin (nen) .... skier
der Skilehrer (-) .... ski instructor
die Skilehrerin (nen) .... ski instructor

Der Wintersportort Ski resort
der Berg (e) .... mountain
die Eisbahn (en) .... ice rink
der Gletscher (-) .... glacier
das Gletschertaxi (s) .... snowmobile
der Hang (Hänge) .... slope
die Hütte (n) .... mountain refuge,
                     bothy
die Lawine (n) .... avalanche
die Piste (n) .... piste, ski run
der Schnee .... snow
der Schneeball (-bälle) . snowball

die Schneeflocke (n) .... snowflake

der Schneemann (-männer) ... snowman

der Schneepflug (-pflüge) ..... snow-plough

der Schneesturm (-stürme) .... snowstorm

die Seilbahn (en) .... cable car

die Sesselbahn (en) ...... chair lift

das Skigeschäft (e) .... ski shop

der Skilift (s) .... ski lift

das Snowboarding........ snowboarding

die Tellerbahn (en) ...... ski lift

Skiausrüstung   **Skiing equipment**

der Handschuh (e)........ glove

die Mütze (n).............. hat

die Salopette (n) .... salopette

die Skibrille (n) .... pair of ski goggles

die Skier *pl*.................. skis

die Skihose (n) .... ski pants

die Skistiefel *pl*............ ski boots

der Skistock (-stöcke) .. ski pole

Ausflüge   Outings

Safaripark   **Safari park**

der Fisch (e) .... fish

das Reptil (ien) .... reptile

das Tier (e) .... animal

der Vogel (Vögel)........ bird

die Kralle (n).............. claw

die Pfote (n) .... paw

der Rüssel (-) .... trunk (elephant)

die Schnauze (n)......... muzzle, snout

der Schwanz (Schwänze) . tail

der Affe (n) *wk* .... monkey

der Bär (en) *wk* .... bear

der Eisbär (en) *wk*........ polar bear

der Elefant (en) *wk* ...... elephant

die Giraffe (n) .... giraffe

das Kamel (e)............. camel

das Krokodil (e) .... crocodile

der Löwe (n) *wk*.......... lion

die Löwin (nen).......... lioness

das Nilpferd (e) .... rhinoceros

der Otter (-)................. otter

der Schimpanse (n)...... chimpanzee

die Schlange (n) .... snake

der Seehund (e) .... seal

der Tiger (-)................. tiger

der Wolf (Wölfe)........ wolf

das Zebra (s)............... zebra

Feld und Wald   **Farm and woodland**

das Feld (er) .... field

die Scheune (n) .... barn

der Stall (Ställe) .... stable

der Bulle (n) *wk*.......... bull

das Eichhörnchen (-).... squirrel

die Ente (n) .... duck

der Esel (-) .... donkey

der Frosch (Frösche).... frog

der Fuchs (Füchse) ...... fox

die Gans (Gänse)......... goose

der Hahn (Hähne)........ cockerel

das Huhn (Hühner) ...... hen

der Hund (e) .... dog

der Igel (-) .... hedgehog

das Kalb (Kälber) .... calf

das Kaninchen (-) .... rabbit

die Katze (n) .... cat

die Kröte (n)............... toad

das Küken (-).............. chick

die Kuh (e) .... cow

das Lamm (Lämmer) ... lamb

die Maus (Mäuse)........ mouse

der Ochse (n) *wk*.......... bullock

das Pferd (e) .... horse

die Ratte (n) .... rat

das Schaf (e)............... sheep

das Schwein (e) .... pig

der Truthahn (-hähne).. turkey

die Ziege (n)............... goat

For insects see page 85

Picknick — Picnic

Wohin gehst du?	**Where are you going?**
an den Strand	to the beach
aufs Land	into the country
in die Berge	into the mountains
in die Wälder	into the woods
zum Rastplatz	to the picnic area

For weather see page 49
For food and drink see pages 23, 53, 78

Wie war das?	**What was it like?**
beliebt	popular
bequem	comfortable
besetzt	taken, occupied
bildschön	picturesque
billig	cheap
das ganze Jahr	all year round
fantastisch	fantastic
friedlich	peaceful
nicht gestattet	not allowed
groß	big
historisch	historic
hübsch	pretty
inbegriffen	included
laut	noisy
luxuriös	luxurious
zum Mitnehmen	take away
pflicht *inv*	compulsory
privat	private
ruhig	peaceful
im Schatten	shady
schön	beautiful
sonnig	sunny
voll	full
wunderbar	superb

Nützliche Verben	**Useful verbs**
sich amüsieren †	to have a good time
besichtigen †	to visit (place)
besuchen †	to visit (person)
bezahlen †	to pay (for)
bleiben* *irreg*	to stay

in Urlaub fahren* *irreg*	to go on holiday
gehen* *irreg*	to go
zu Fuß gehen* *irreg*	to walk
helfen (+ dat) *irreg*	to help
kochen	to cook
kosten †	to cost
laufen* *irreg*	to walk; to run
losfahren* *irreg sep*	to set out
öffnen †	to open
reisen*	to travel
reiten* *irreg*	to ride
schließen *irreg*	to close
schwimmen(*) *irreg*	to swim, bathe
sehen *irreg*	to see
auf Urlaub sein* *irreg*	to be on holiday
spazieren gehen* *irreg sep*	to go for a walk
spielen	to play
suchen	to look for

ein Zelt abbauen *sep*	to pack up a tent
ein Zelt aufbauen *sep*	to pitch a tent
baden †	to bathe
sich bedanken † (bei + dat)	to thank
ertrinken* *irreg*	to drown
Schlitten fahren* *irreg*	to go sledging
Wasserski fahren* *irreg*	to water ski
bergsteigen gehen* *irreg*	to go mountaineering
Winterurlaub machen	to take a winter holiday
ein Picknick mitnehmen *irreg sep*	to take a picnic
rudern	to row
segeln	to sail
seekrank sein* *irreg*	to be seasick
Ski laufen* *sep irreg*	to ski
sich sonnen	to sunbathe
surfen	to surf
tauchen*	to dive
14 Tage verbringen *irreg*	to spend a fortnight
verleihen *irreg*	to hire, let
wandern*	to go for a hike
windsurfen	to sailboard
zelten †	to camp

Redewendungen

Ich habe die Sommerferien am Meer verbracht *I spent the summer holidays by the sea*

Letztes Jahr habe ich Deutschland besucht *I visited Germany last year*

Wir haben in Österreich gezeltet *We went camping in Austria*

Ich war mit meiner Familie unterwegs *I went with my family*

Wir haben vierzehn Tage in den Bergen verbracht *We spent a fortnight in the mountains*

In den Osterferien werde ich in die Schweiz fahren *I shall be going to Switzerland in the Easter holidays*

Zu Weihnachten werde ich in Obergurgl Ski laufen *I shall be going skiing in Obergurgl at Christmas*

Ich möchte ein Zimmer mit Bad für zwei Personen reservieren, bitte *I would like to reserve a room, with a bath, for two people*

Wir haben vor, zwei Nächte zu bleiben *We are planning to stay three nights*

Wann gibt es Frühstück, bitte? *What time is breakfast?*

Wo kann ich das Auto parken, bitte? *Where may I park the car, please?*

Die Seife ist alle *There is no soap left*

Gibt es ein Restaurant hier in der Nähe? *Is there a restaurant nearby?*

DIE INTERNATIONALE WELT

Allgemeines   General

die Aggression (en) ..... aggression

der Analphabetismus.... illiteracy

die Armut .... poverty

das Asyl .... political asylum

der Asylbewerber (-).... asylum seeker

der Aussiedler (-) .... German-speaking
immigrant

die Bestechung .... corruption

die Entwicklungsländer *pl*
.... developing countries

der Flüchtling (e) .... refugee

der Gastarbeiter (-) ...... foreign worker

die Geheimpolizei........ secret police

die Gleichberechtigung equal rights

die Hautfarbe (n) .... skin colour

der übernationale Konzern
.... multinational company

die Krankheit (en)........ illness

die geistige Krankheit (en)
.... psychiatric illness

die entwickelten Länder *pl*
.... developed countries

die industrialisierten Länder *pl*
.... industrialised countries

die reichen Länder *pl* ... rich countries

der Obdachlose (n) ‡ ... homeless person

die Religion (en).......... religion

die politische Überzeugung... political opinion

das Vorurteil (e).......... prejudice

die Dritte Welt............ the Third World

Nützliche Verben   Useful verbs

ausüben *sep* .... to exploit

Selbstmord begehen *irreg* to commit suicide

Asyl gewähren † .... to give asylum to

Verständnis für etwas haben *irreg*
.................to have an understanding of sthg

quälen......................... to torture

respektieren † .... to have respect for

töten † .... to kill

Geschichte und Politik
History and politics

Leute   People

der Abgeordnete (n) ‡.. MP

die Arbeiterklasse (n) .. working class

der Bundeskanzler (-) .. Chancellor

die Demokratie (n) ...... democracy

die Deutschen ‡.......... the Germans

der Frieden .... peace

der Kapitalismus......... capitalism

der Kommunismus ...... communism

der König (e).............. king

die Königin (en) .... queen

der Krieg (e)............... war

das Land (Länder) .... country

die Mittelschicht......... middle classes

die Monarchie (n)........ monarchy

die Nation (en) .... nation

die öffentliche Meinung .. public opinion

das Parlament (e)........ parliament

die politische Partei (en).. party (political)

der Präsident (en) *wk* ... president

der Premierminister (-) Prime Minister

die Prinzessin (en) .... princess

der Prinz (en) *wk* .... prince

die Queen .... Queen Elizabeth II

die Regierung (en)....... government

die Republik (en)......... republic

die Revolution (en)...... revolution

der Sozialismus .... socialism

der Staat (en) .... state

der Zivilkrieg (e) .... civil war

der erste Weltkrieg ...... World War 1

der zweite Weltkrieg.... World War 2

Geographie   Geography

der Berg (e) .... mountain

das Dorf (Dörfer)......... village

die Ebene (n).............. plain

der Felsen (-) .... cliff
der Fluss (Flüsse)........ river (large)
das Gebiet (e).............. region
das Gebirge.................. mountain range
der Gipfel (-) .... peak
die Hochebene (n) .... plateau
der Hügel (-).............. hill
der Kanal (Kanäle) ...... canal
der Kontinent (e) .... continent
das Land (Länder)........ country
der Regenwald (-wälder) . rain forest
die Stadt (Städte)......... town
das Tal (Täler) .... valley

Umweltschutz   Conservation

die Auswirkung (en).... effect
die Energie.................. energy
die Erde (n) .... earth
die Folge (n)................ consequence
der Grund (Gründe) ..... reason
die Natur .... nature
der Planet (en) *wk* .... planet
die Sonne (n) .... sun
die Welt...................... world
der Weltraum............... space
die Zukunft.................. future

das Blatt (Blätter)......... leaf
die Fauna (Faunen)...... animals, fauna
die Flora (Floren) .... plants, flora
das Klima (s) .... climate
das Ökosystem (e)........ ecosystem
die Ozonschicht (en).... ozone layer
der Vogelschutz........... protection of birds
die Umwelt.................. environment
der Wald (Wälder)....... forest
die Wüste (n).............. wilderness, desert

Unglücke   Disasters

das Abschmelzen .... thawing
der Brand (Brände) ...... fire
die Dürre.................... drought
die Entwaldung .... deforestation

die Epidemie (n)........ epidemic
das Erdbeben (-) .... earthquake
die Explosion (en) .... explosion
die Flutwelle (n).......... tidal wave
die Hungersnot........... famine
die Klimaveränderung (en)
.... climate change
die Lawine (n)............. avalanche
das Ozonloch (-löcher) hole in the ozone layer
die Stadtverschmutzung ....urban pollution
der Treibhauseffekt ....greenhouse effect
die Überschwemmung (en)....flood
der Vulkanausbruch..... volcanic eruption
das Waldsterben .... forest death
der Wirbelsturm .... tornado

Umweltverschmutzer
Sources of pollution

die Abgase .... exhaust gases
das Auspuffrohr (-röhre)...exhaust pipe
die Braunkohle........... brown coal
der Brennstoff (e) .... fuel
das Erdgas .... natural gas
die Fabrik (en)............ factory
der FCKW.................. CFC
das Holz .... wood
die chemischen Industrien ..chemical industries
das Kernkraftwerk (e).. nuclear power station
die Kohle (n).............. coal
die Kohlenindustrie ..... coal industry
das Kraftwerk (e)........ power station
die Ölraffinerie (n) ...... oil refinery
der Öltanker (-) .... oil tanker
der Ölteppich (e) .... oil slick
die Pestizide (n) .... pesticide
der radioaktive Niederschlag
.... radioactive fall-out
der saure Regen........... acid rain
die Säure .... acid
die Schlackenhalde (n) slag heap
Tschernobyl.......... Chernobyl
der Verkehr .... traffic

Haushaltsmüll   Domestic waste

das Altglascontainer (-) bottle bank
das Altpapier............... recycled paper
die Aludose (n) .... aluminium can
die Batterie (n) .... battery
die Einwegflasche (n) .. non-returnable bottle
das Glas (Gläser).......... glass
der Kunststoff (e)......... plastic
das Metall (e).............. metal
der Müll...................... domestic waste
das Papier .... paper
die Pfandflasche (n)..... returnable bottle
die Plastiktüte (n) .... plastic bag
das Recycling.............. recycling
die Stahldose (n).......... steel can

braun .... brown
grün............................ green
klar............................ clear
schädlich .... harmful
vergiftet...................... poisoned
wiederverwendbar .... re-usable

Lebewesen   Fauna

Insekten   Insects

die Ameise (n) .... ant
die Biene (n)............... bee
die Fliege (n) .... fly
der Marienkäfer (-) ...... ladybird
die Motte (n) .... moth
die Mücke (n) .... mosquito
die Raupe (n) .... caterpillar
der Schmetterling (e) ... butterfly
die Spinne (n) .... spider
die Wespe (n) .... wasp

Vögel   Birds

die Eule (n)................. owl
der Raubvogel (-vögel) bird of prey
der Schwan (Schwäne). swan
der Zugvogel (-vögel) .. migratory bird

Tiere   Animals

eine vom Aussterben bedrohte Art (en)
.... endangered species
der Blauwal (e)........... blue whale
der Delphin (e) .... dolphin
der Eisbär (en) *wk*....... polar bear
der Hai (e) .... shark
der Orang-Utan (s) ...... orang-utan
der Panda (s) .... giant panda
For other animals see page 30

das Elfenbein............... ivory
das Fell....................... fur
das Futter.................... fodder
das Habitat (e) .... habitat
die Leiche (n).............. corpse
das Plankton *no pl* .... plankton
der Stoßzahn (-zähne).. tusk

Flora   Flora

der Baum (Bäume) ...... tree
die Blume (n) .... flower
die Eiche (n)............... oak
die Kiefer (n).............. pine tree
der Tannenbaum (-bäume)..fir tree
der Wald (Wälder)....... wood, forest

Adjektive   Adjectives

chemisch .... chemical
feucht .... humid
heiß........................... hot
kalt........................... cold
Kern~........................ nuclear
laut .... noisy
nass .... wet
ökologisch.................. ecological
schädlich .... harmful
schrecklich .... awful
städtisch .... urban
steil .... steep
strafbar...................... criminal
trüb .... dark, gloomy

umweltfeindlich.......... environmentally damaging	recyceln †.................... to recycle
umweltfreundlich .... environmentally friendly	sammeln...................... to collect, pick (flowers)
verletzt .... injured, wounded	schonen...................... to protect from harm
weich.......................... soft, gentle	schützen .... to conserve, protect
	sparen......................... to save

Nützliche Verben   **Useful verbs**

abladen *irreg sep* .... to dump at sea (oil, chemicals)	stehlen *irreg* .... to steal
	steigen* *irreg* .... to rise (temperature)
atmen †....................... to breathe	töten † .... to kill
ausplündern *sep* .... to exploit	überschreiten *irreg insep* ..to exceed
austrocknen † *sep* .... to parch, dry out	verbessern † .... to improve
bebauen † .... to grow, cultivate	verbreiten † .... to spread
bedrohen †................... to threaten	verbrennen *irreg*.......... to burn
beeinflussen †.............. to influence	vergiften †.................. to poison
beschädigen † .... to damage	vermeiden *irreg*........... to avoid
fallen* *irreg*................ to fall (temperature)	verschmutzen † .... to pollute
leiden *irreg* an (+ dat).. to suffer from	verschwenden †.......... to waste
	verurteilen † .... to condemn
	zerstören †.................. to destroy

86

LÄNDER, REGIONEN, STÄDTE

Die Europäische Union (EU)   The European Union

Land	Bedeutung	Einwohner	Einwohnerin	Adjektiv
Country	*Meaning*	*Inhabitant*	*Inhabitant*	*Adjective*
England	*England*	der Engländer(-)	die Engländerin(nen)	englisch
Irland	*Irish Republic*	der Ire(n)	die Irin(nen)	irisch
Nordirland	*N Ireland*	der Ire(n)	die Irin(nen)	irisch
Schottland	*Scotland*	der Schotte(n)	die Schottin(nen)	schottisch
Wales	*Wales*	der Waliser(-)	die Waliserin(nen)	walisisch
Deutschland	*Germany*	der Deutsche(n)	die Deutsche(n)	deutsch
Österreich	*Austria*	der Österreicher(-)	die Österreicherin(nen)	österreichisch
Belgien	*Belgium*	der Belgier(-)	die Belgierin(nen)	belgisch
Dänemark	*Denmark*	der Däne(n)	die Dänin(nen)	dänisch
Spanien	*Spain*	der Spanier(-)	die Spanierin(nen)	spanisch
Finnland	*Finland*	der Finnländer(-)	die Finnländerin(nen)	finnländisch
Frankreich	*France*	der Franzose(n)	die Französin(nen)	französisch
Griechenland	*Greece*	der Grieche(n)	die Griechin(nen)	griechisch
Italien	*Italy*	der Italiener(-)	die Italienerin(nen)	italienisch
Luxemburg	*Luxembourg*	der Luxemburger(-)	die Luxemburgerin(nen)	luxemburgisch
die Niederlande	*Netherlands*	der Niederländer(-)	die Niederländerin(nen)	niederländisch
Portugal	*Portugal*	der Portugiese(n)	die Portugiesin(nen)	portugiesisch
Schweden	*Sweden*	der Schwede(n)	die Schwedin(nen)	schwedisch

Andere Länder   Other Countries

Afrika	*Africa*	der Afrikaner(-)	die Afrikanerin(nen)	afrikanisch
Amerika	*America*	der Amerikaner(-)	der Amerikanerin(nen)	amerikanisch
Australien	*Australia*	der Australier(-)	die Australierin(nen)	australisch
Europa	*Europe*	der Europäer(-)	die Europäerin(nen)	europäisch
Russland	*Russia*	der Russe(n)	die Russin(nen)	russisch
die Schweiz	*Switzerland*	der Schweizer(-)	die Schweizerin(nen)	schweizerisch

Eigennamen   Proper names

Bayern .... Bavaria

der Bodensee .... Lake Constance

Brügge .... Bruges

Brüssel .... Brussels

die Donau .... the Danube

Genf .... Geneva

der Kanal .... the English Channel

Köln .... Cologne

Lüttich .... Liège

das Mittelmeer .... Mediterranean

die Mosel .... the Moselle

Moskau.................. Moscow

München .... Munich

die Nordsee .... North Sea

die Ostsee................... Baltic Sea

der Rhein................... the Rhine

die Themse................ the Thames

Venedig............... Venice

Warschau.............. Warsaw

Wien.................... Vienna

ZAHLEN, DATEN, UHRZEITEN

Kardinalzahlen		Cardinal Numbers	
0	null	10	zehn
1	eins	11	elf
2	zwei	12	zwölf
3	drei	13	dreizehn
4	vier	14	vierzehn
5	fünf	15	fünfzehn
6	sechs	16	sechzehn *NB spelling*
7	sieben	17	siebzehn *NB spelling*
8	acht	18	achtzehn
9	neun	19	neunzehn

20	zwanzig
21	einundzwanzig *NB spelling*
22	zweiundzwanzig, etc

30	dreißig *NB spelling*
40	vierzig
50	fünfzig
60	sechzig *NB spelling*
70	siebzig *NB spelling*
80	achtzig
90	neunzig
100	hundert
101	hunderteins
102	hundertzwei
141	hunderteinundvierzig
200	zweihundert
999	neunhundertneunundneunzig
1000	tausend
1100	tausendeinhundert/elfhundert/eintausendeinhundert
321 456	dreihunderteinundzwanzigtausendvierhundertsechsundfünfzig
1 000 000	eine Million (spaces every 3 digits, no commas)

Remember that:

1 Years are usually stated in hundreds.
   So 1999 = neunzehnhundertneunundneunzig

2 Where there is any danger of confusion, *zwo* is used instead of *zwei*.
   It is often heard in public announcements, and on the telephone.

3 Longer numbers - such as telephone numbers after dialling codes - are often
   written and read in pairs. So 01684/57 74 33 is pronounced as:
   Null eins sechs acht vier, siebenundfünfzig vierundsiebzig dreiunddreißig.

4 Cardinal numbers can be used as nouns, particularly when discussing school
   grades.
   Example: Ich habe eine Eins in Mathe *I have a 1 in maths*

Ordinalzahlen

der erste	first
der zweite	second
der dritte	third
der vierte	fourth
der fünfte	fifth
der sechste	sixth
der siebte	seventh
der achte	eighth
der neunte	ninth
der zehnte	tenth
der elfte	eleventh

Ordinal numbers

der zwölfte	twelfth
der dreizehnte	thirteenth
der vierzehnte	fourteenth
der fünfzehnte	fifteenth
der sechzehnte	sixteenth
der siebzehnte	seventeenth
der achtzehnte	eighteenth
der neunzehnte	nineteenth
der zwanzigste	twentieth
der einundzwanzigste	twenty-first
der zweiundzwanzigste	twenty-second

Tage und Monate

All of these are masculine.

Days and months

Montag	*Monday*	Freitag	*Friday*
Dienstag	*Tuesday*	Samstag	*Saturday*
Mittwoch	*Wednesday*	Sonnabend	*Saturday*
Donnerstag	*Thursday*	Sonntag	*Sunday*

Januar	*January*	Juli	*July*
Februar	*February*	August	*August*
März	*March*	September	*September*
April	*April*	Oktober	*October*
Mai	*May*	November	*November*
Juni	*June*	Dezember	*December*

am Montag   *on Monday*   **im** Februar   *in February*

When there is any danger of confusion, *Juno* is used for *Juni* and *Julei* for *Juli*.

Daten   Dates

Heute haben wir den ersten September	Today is September 1st
Heute haben wir den zweiten Januar	Today is January 2nd
Heute haben wir den siebten März	Today is March 7th
Heute haben wir den fünfundzwanzigsten Mai	Today is May 25th
Heute haben wir den dreißigsten April	Today is April 30th
Ich habe am vierten Februar Geburtstag	My birthday is February 4th
Ich bin 1984 geboren	I was born in 1984

Remember that 'in' is **not** used with years in German.

Die Uhrzeiten

Clock Times

In German, as in English, there are two ways of telling the time, the everyday way and using the 24-hour clock.

Everyday way		24-hour clock	
Es ist ein Uhr	1.00	Es ist ein Uhr	01.00
Es ist fünf Uhr	5.00	Es ist fünf Uhr	05.00
Es ist fünf (Minuten) nach fünf	5.05	Es ist siebzehn Uhr	17.00
Es ist Viertel nach fünf	5.15	Es ist siebzehn Uhr fünf	17.05
Es ist halb sechs (*careful!*)	5.30	Es ist siebzehn Uhr fünfzehn	17.15
Es ist Viertel vor sechs	5.45	Es ist siebzehn Uhr dreißig	17.30
Es ist fünf (Minuten) vor sechs	5.55	Es ist siebzehn Uhr fünfundvierzig	17.45
Es ist Mittag/Mitternacht	12.00	Es ist siebzehn Uhr fünfundfünfzig	17.55
Es ist Viertel nach zwölf	12.15	Es ist zwölf Uhr	12.00
		Es ist null Uhr eins	00.01

Wann?

When?

vor einem Jahr..............	a year ago
letzte Woche.................	last week
jeden Tag.....................	every day
vorgestern...................	the day before yesterday
gestern........................	yesterday
gestern Abend..............	last night
heute...........................	today
am Vormittag	in the morning

am Nachmittag.............	in the afternoon
am Abend.....................	in the evening
morgen........................	tomorrow
morgen früh	tomorrow morning
übermorgen.................	the day after tomorrow
nächste Woche	next week
nächstes Jahr	next year
in zwei Jahren..............	in two years' time

Verbs with separable or inseparable prefixes and with the prefixes *be-*, *ent-*, *er-*, *ge-* and *ver-* should be looked up without their prefix. * denotes verb with *sein* in perfect and other compound tenses.

Infinitive	3rd Person Present	Imperfect	Perfect	Meaning
backen	**bäckt**	backte	gebacken	*to bake*
befehlen	**befiehlt**	befahl	befohlen	*to command*
begießen	begießt	begoss	begossen	*to water (plants)*
beginnen	beginnt	begann	begonnen	*to begin*
beißen	beißt	biss	gebissen	*to bite*
bersten	**birst**	barst	geborsten*	*to burst*
beschließen	beschließt	beschloss	beschlossen	*to decide*
beschreiben	beschreibt	beschrieb	beschrieben	*to describe*
biegen	biegt	bog	gebogen	*to bend*
bieten	**bietet**	bot	geboten	*to offer*
binden	**bindet**	band	gebunden	*to fasten*
bitten (um)	**bittet (um)**	bat (um)	gebeten	*to ask (for)*
blasen	**bläst**	blies	geblasen	*to blow*
bleiben	bleibt	blieb	geblieben*	*to stay*
braten	**brät**	briet	gebraten	*to roast*
brechen	**bricht**	brach	gebrochen	*to break*
brennen	brennt	brannte	gebrannt	*to burn*
bringen	bringt	brachte	gebracht	*to bring*

Unregelmäßige Verben

Infinitive	3rd Person Present	Imperfect	Perfect	Meaning
denken	denkt	dachte	gedacht	to think
dürfen	darf	durfte		to be allowed to
empfehlen	empfiehlt	empfahl	empfohlen	to recommend
erschrecken	erschrickt	erschrak	erschrocken	to terrify
essen	isst	aß	gegessen	to eat
fahren	fährt	fuhr	gefahren*	to travel
fallen	fällt	fiel	gefallen*	to fall
fangen	fängt	fing	gefangen	to catch
finden	findet	fand	gefunden	to find
fliegen	fliegt	flog	geflogen*	to fly
frieren	friert	fror	gefroren	to freeze
geben	gibt	gab	gegeben	to give
gehen	geht	ging	gegangen*	to go
gelingen	gelingt	gelang	gelungen*	to succeed
genießen	genießt	genoss	genossen	to enjoy
geschehen	geschieht	geschah	geschehen*	to happen
gewinnen	gewinnt	gewann	gewonnen	to win
greifen	greift	griff	gegriffen	to grasp
haben	hat	hatte	gehabt	to have
halten	hält	hielt	gehalten	to stop, to hold
hängen	hängt	hing	gehangen	to hang

Infinitive	3rd Person Present	Imperfect	Perfect	Meaning
heben	hebt	hob	gehoben	to lift
heißen	heißt	hieß	geheißen	to be called
helfen	**hilft**	half	geholfen	to help
kennen	kennt	kannte	gekannt	to know
kommen	kommt	kam	gekommen*	to come
können	**kann**	konnte		to be able to
laden	**lädt**	lud	geladen	to load
lassen	**lässt**	ließ	gelassen	to leave
laufen	**läuft**	lief	gelaufen*	to run
leiden	**leidet**	litt	gelitten	to suffer
leihen	leiht	lieh	geliehen	to lend
lesen	**liest**	las	gelesen	to read
liegen	liegt	lag	gelegen	to lie
liegen lassen	lässt liegen	ließ liegen	liegen lassen	to leave lying around
messen	**misst**	maß	gemessen	to measure
mögen	**mag**	mochte		to like to
müssen	**muss**	musste		to have to
nehmen	**nimmt**	nahm	genommen	to take
nennen	nennt	nannte	genannt	to name
pfeifen	pfeift	pfiff	gepfiffen	to whistle
raten	**rät**	riet	geraten	to guess

Unregelmäßige Verben

Infinitive	3rd Person Present	Imperfect	Perfect	Meaning
reiben	reibt	rieb	gerieben	to rub
reißen	reißt	riss	gerissen	to tear
reiten	**reitet**	ritt	geritten*	to ride
riechen	riecht	roch	gerochen	to smell
rufen	ruft	rief	gerufen	to call
scheiden	**scheidet**	schied	geschieden	to part
scheinen	scheint	schien	geschienen	to shine, to seem
schieben	schiebt	schob	geschoben	to push
schießen	schießt	schoss	geschossen	to shoot
schlafen	**schläft**	schlief	geschlafen	to sleep
schlagen	**schlägt**	schlug	geschlagen	to hit
schleichen	schleicht	schlich	geschlichen*	to creep
schließen	schließt	schloss	geschlossen	to shut
schneiden	**schneidet**	schnitt	geschnitten	to cut
schreiben	schreibt	schrieb	geschrieben	to write
schreien	schreit	schrie	geschrieen	to shout
schweigen	schweigt	schwieg	geschwiegen	to be silent
schwimmen	schwimmt	schwamm	geschwommen(*)	to swim
sehen	**sieht**	sah	gesehen	to see
sein	**ist**	war	gewesen*	to be
singen	singt	sang	gesungen	to sing

94

Infinitive	3rd Person Present	Imperfect	Perfect	Meaning
sinken	sinkt	sank	gesunken*	to sink
sitzen	sitzt	saß	gesessen	to sit
sollen	**soll**	sollte		to be supposed to, to ought to
sprechen	**spricht**	sprach	gesprochen	to speak
springen	springt	sprang	gesprungen*	to jump
stechen	**sticht**	stoch	gestochen	to sting
stehen	steht	stand	gestanden	to stand
stehlen	**stiehlt**	stahl	gestohlen	to steal
sterben	**stirbt**	starb	gestorben*	to die
steigen	steigt	stieg	gestiegen*	to climb
stinken	stinkt	stank	gestunken	to smell
stoßen	**stößt**	stieß	gestoßen*	to bump
streichen	streicht	strich	gestrichen	to cancel
sich streiten	**streitet**	stritt	gestritten	to argue
tragen	**trägt**	trug	getragen	to carry, to wear
treffen	**trifft**	traf	getroffen	to meet, to hit
treiben	treibt	trieb	getrieben	to do (sport)
treten	**tritt**	trat	getreten*	to step
trinken	trinkt	trank	getrunken	to drink
tun	**tut**	tat	getan	to do

Unregelmäßige Verben

Infinitive	3rd Person Present	Imperfect	Perfect	Meaning
verbringen	verbringt	verbrachte	verbracht	to spend time
vergessen	**vergisst**	vergaß	vergessen	to forget
vergleichen	vergleicht	verglich	verglichen	to compare
verlassen	**verlässt**	verließ	verlassen	to leave
verlieren	verliert	verlor	verloren	to lose
vermeiden	**vermeidet**	vermied	vermieden	to avoid
verschleißen	verschleißt	verschliss	verschlissen	to wear out
verschwinden	**verschwindet**	verschwand	verschwunden*	to disappear
wachsen	**wächst**	wuchs	gewachsen*	to grow
waschen	**wäscht**	wusch	gewaschen	to wash
weisen	weist	wies	gewiesen	to show
werben	wirbt	warb	geworben	to advertise
werden	**wird**	wurde	geworden*	to become
werfen	**wirft**	warf	geworfen	to throw
wiegen	wiegt	wog	gewogen	to weigh
wissen	**weiß**	wusste	gewusst	to know
wollen	**will**	wollte		to want to
ziehen	zieht	zog	gezogen	to pull
zwingen	zwingt	zwang	gezwungen	to force